THE ROUGH GUIDE to the

iPad

by

Peter Buckley

ROUGH GUIDES

www.roughguides.com

Credits

The Rough Guide to the iPad

Text and design: Peter Buckley
Editing and layout: Kate Berens
Proofreading: Susanne Hillen
Production: Gemma Sharpe

Rough Guides Reference

Director: Andrew Lockett
Editors: Kate Berens, Tom Cabot,
Tracy Hopkins, Matthew Milton,
Joe Staines

Publishing information

This third edition published August 2012 by
Rough Guides Ltd, 80 Strand, London, WC2R 0RL
Email: mail@roughguides.com

Distributed by the Penguin Group:
Penguin Books Ltd, 80 Strand, London, WC2R 0RL
Penguin Group (USA), 375 Hudson Street, NY 10014, USA
Penguin Group (Australia), 250 Camberwell Road, Camberwell, Victoria 3124, Australia
Penguin Group (New Zealand), Cnr Rosedale and Airborne Roads, Albany, Auckland, New Zealand

Rough Guides is represented in Canada by Tourmaline Editions Inc., 662 King Street West, Suite 304,
Toronto, Ontario, M5V 1M7

Printed in Singapore by Toppan Security Printing Pte. Ltd.
Typeset in Minion, Myriad and Proxima Nova

iPad cover images photographed by Mark Thomas

272 pages; includes index

A catalogue record for this book is available from the British Library.

ISBN: 978-1-40936-394-1

1 3 5 7 9 8 6 4 2

For Rosalie

Contents

Music & video

Reading

The internet

Navigation & travel

App essentials

Maintenance

Introduction

A lot of people asked me why I was writing a book on the iPad. Surely there's not enough to say, now that everyone's so used to iPods and iPhones? And what about the internet? Isn't everything we need to know available online?

And yet, many of these same people followed on with a rally of questions about the device. Does it feel heavy to hold? What's the score with the non-replaceable battery? Should I go for the Wi-Fi or 3G/4G model? Do I really need a Retina screen? Is the iPad better than other tablet options?

There's lots of misinformation about, and rather than filtering through all the "noise" of the internet, people wanted a one-stop shop for answers, advice and suggestions. That's what I hope you'll be getting here: a couple of hundred pages of tips, tricks and answers to all those nagging questions that pop up before you buy a device like the iPad, and when you turn the thing on for the first time. And then answers to a whole bunch of questions that you didn't even know you wanted to ask.

The iPad is already revolutionizing the way people think about their digital lifestyles. It's the device that cements the idea that computing isn't just about number-crunching, but is about the things we do every day around the home and out and about. Just think about the possibilities for this kind of device: it offers a whole new way to enjoy the internet; you can prop it up in the kitchen to follow a recipe; relax in bed with a favourite novel or the latest news; show photos to friends in the pub; tap out a few emails; even knock out a spreadsheet. The list is seemingly endless, and it isn't hard to imagine a not-too-distant future where there are iPads lying around every home.

The fact that you're reading this shows you're interested in the iPad. You may well have bought one already. You might even be reading this on its screen (just as I am writing this on its screen). For a moment, however, let's assume you're one of the many people who don't get what all the fuss is about. Well, it's an Apple product for a start, and that's reason enough to make a fuss in some circles. Apple don't tend to release a product unless the time is right and the experience is absolutely cracking. When the first iPad appeared, in 2010, it was most certainly the right time for a reinvention of the personal computer, and touchscreen technology is proving itself the undisputed successor to the mouse and keyboard. A couple of years later and there are already a lot of wannabe-iPad tablet computers in the shops, though few come close when sat alongside even Apple's first-generation model. With the launch of the impressive third-generation design, dubbed simply "The New iPad" at the time of launch, Apple's tablet is once again ahead of the curve.

So, what can you expect when you get the iPad out of the box for the first time? After the initial "wow" moment, expect a couple of days of mild confusion… It isn't necessarily obvious how this device is going to fit into your daily life. But any doubts soon pass as you find yourself using the iPad more and more – and that's where this book will help, hooking you up with the best apps and showing you all the most useful tips and tricks.

If there's one thing you'll learn during these first few weeks, it's that the iPad is a blank canvas, and with the right apps installed, the possibilities are limitless…

About this book

Text written like **this** denotes a command or label as it appears on either a computer's screen or the iPad's screen. There are also many coloured buttons and icons used within these pages, such as this ⊖ and this ⊚ which relate to buttons and icons as they appeared on the iPad's screen at the time of writing.

   This book was written using an iPad running iOS 5.1. (To see which version you're running, look within **Settings > General** and then look for the line marked **Version.**) If you're running a later version of iOS then you may well come across features not covered here, though the majority of what's written will still apply.

Acknowledgements

Thanks go to Kate Berens, Andrew Lockett and everyone at Rough Guides who helped get this book together in record time. Also to Duncan, Joe and Jonathan for their camaraderie, and a special shout to Roz, Claire, Paul, Stu, James and Alex – I couldn't have done it without you all around me making work so much fun. And a special thanks to my wife and daughter for their endless supply of encouragement, coffee and toast.

Primer

01

FAQs

**Everything you ever wanted
to know but were afraid to ask**

The big picture

What's an iPad?

In Apple's eye, the iPad is the missing link between the iPhone and their MacBook (laptop) range. It's a tablet computer that offers the best of both worlds: the touchscreen and breadth of activities of a smartphone (web browsing, email, etc), but with a size and computing power verging on that of some laptops. It can also play music, movies and video and display eBooks. Add to this the ability to play videogames and install applications (or apps), and you have a pretty impressive device.

The iPad was launched in April 2010 in the US, and elsewhere soon after. The second-generation iPad appeared in spring 2011, boasting two integrated cameras, a faster, more powerful spec and a choice of black or white bezels. With the third-generation iPad, launched March 2012, came a high-definition Retina display, another boost in processing power, better built-in cameras and the addition of dictation functionality (though not the full Siri voice interaction service that made its way onto the iPhone at the end of 2011).

Is the iPad the only device of this kind?

Tablet computers (flat computing devices with an interactive screen making up the majority of one face) are not new, but the iPad was the first to really capture the public imagination and demonstrate the potential of tablets.

There are now dozens of tablet devices on the market, many of them running Google's Android operating system. Perhaps the most interesting are the large-screened Motorola Xoom and the Samsung Galaxy Tab and Galaxy Note devices.

The Apple Newton

Long before the iPad, or even the iPod, showed its face, there was the Newton … Apple's first venture into the world of tablet computing. The project kicked off in 1989, and for the next decade the various Newton incarnations wholeheartedly failed to capture the public's imagination, though they did find a home amongst a select set of business users. Unlike the iPad, the Newtons used a stylus rather than a finger for input, and also featured handwriting recognition technology (sadly missing as a built-in feature of the first-generation iPads). By the end of the 1990s, the Newton project had been terminated, but its influence remained, and the years since witnessed near-constant speculation about when Apple would again embrace tablet computing.

EBook readers, such as Amazon's Kindle (you can choose between the easy-on-the-eye E Ink version, or the colour, Android-running Kindle Fire), are also often judged alongside the iPad. However, even though the Kindle Fire can run apps, access the internet, and so on, it doesn't have anywhere near the power of even the first-generation iPad. That said, it is around half the price, and if reading is your prime concern, it does a good job.

How does it compare to the iPhone and iPod touch?

Well, for a start, it's bigger in terms of physical dimensions, but the same as the iPhone when looking at storage capacity. At the time of writing, Apple iPhones and the third-generation iPad are available with capacities of 16, 32 or 64GB of storage space (less around 1GB, which accounts for the operating system, or OS). If you are in the market for an iPod touch, you can choose from 8, 32 or 64GB.

However, it is more interesting to see what other characteristics the iPad shares with its smaller siblings. The main similarity comes in the software and user interface: all run on versions of the same operating system (anchored on the idea of using "apps" for a multitude of activities). Also, these devices all use the same touchscreen technology and language of finger gestures and taps.

Apple's popular Smart Covers magnetically snap to the bodies of both second- and third-generation iPads and come in either leather or polyurethane finishes.

From Apple's perspective, this system works brilliantly. It means that iPhone apps as well as iPad apps will run on the iPad straight out of the box, but, even more significantly, it means that there are millions of people out there who are already familiar with the interface that appears on the iPad. And when you tot up all the iPhone and iPod touch users in the world, that's a lot of potential iPad customers.

So for many, moving to the familiar interface and OS of the iPad will be a very easy transition, while the larger screen size allows for many interesting twists to the user experience that those accustomed to the iPhone and iPod touch already know and love.

To quickly sum it up, the merits of the currently available iPad, besides its slick design, include:

• A large, bright, Retina display screen (2048x1536 pixels) with a resolution of 264 pixels per inch. The iPad 2 boasted half that: 1024x768 pixels, with a resolution of 132 pixels per inch.

• A responsive touchscreen interface that can be understood by almost anyone in a matter of seconds.

• Two built-in cameras (one front-facing, one back-facing), used for video calls (aka FaceTime), photos, shooting video, and more.

• A built-in digital compass and location-aware technology (aka "location services" or "assisted GPS").

• An extremely user-friendly software system.

• An excellent web browser and a top-class email application.

• Compatibility with iTunes on a Mac or PC for syncing content and data via either a cable or over Wi-Fi.

• Wi-Fi (in all models) and 3G and 4G cell network connectivity (in some models) for fast internet access.

• Gigabytes of storage space for movies, music, photos, eBooks, apps, documents and more.

• Loads of downloadable games and applications.

And how big is the third-gen iPad overall?

The Wi-Fi-only model weighs in at 652g (1.44 pounds), while the Wi-Fi+4G version is 662g (1.46 pounds) – that's roughly about the same as the average hardback novel. Both are a little heavier than the second-generation iPads, but not so much that you'd notice. Looked at head-on, the iPad measures a touch under 186mm (7.31 inches) wide and just over 241mm (9.5 inches) tall. And it's 9.4mm (0.37 inches) thick, which is, again, marginally thicker than the iPad 2. Visit apple.com/ipad/specs for more detailed specifications.

Why did Apple skimp on the screen and not make it stretch right to the edges?

Like on the iPhone and iPod touch, you mean? Put simply, you have to be able to hold the thing, and the bevel around the edge gives you somewhere to put your thumbs without obscuring content or confusing the device with unnecessary taps and swipes.

Can I use a stylus instead of my finger?

Let's get technical for a moment … the iPad's screen recognizes your touches in terms of the very specific electrical capacitance of your fingers, and not the actual pressure of your finger as you tap or swipe (as would be the case with most stylus touch systems). That said, there are several stylus devices on the market designed specifically for iPhones, iPods and the iPad. One is the Pogo Sketch – you can find out more at tenonedesign.com/sketch.php. There are also apps that have appeared specifically designed to work with stylus technology. Studio Basic, for example, is a rather fine notes and journalling app designed to be used with Byzero's (pricey) stylus pen. It has a very fine nib, which combined with the app's ability to ignore you resting your hand on the iPad while writing, gives a really nice user experience. Check out by-zero.com, or Amazon, for more info about the hardware.

The other, slightly wackier solution, popular in Korea amongst iPhone users, is to employ a particular brand of snack sausage which displays similar electrostatic characteristics as the human finger – perfect for cold days when you don't want to take your gloves off. For the full story, visit tinyurl.com/yldwb38.

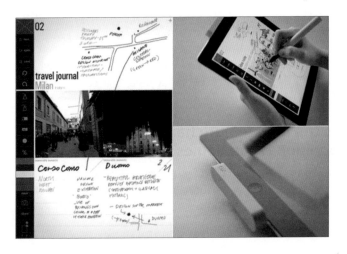

What's iOS and OS X?

All computers have a so-called operating system – the underlying software that acts as a bridge between the hardware, the user and the apps. The standard operating system on PCs is Windows; on Macs, it's OS X.

The operating system on the iPad – known as iOS – is based on OS X, though you wouldn't know it, because it's slimmed down and specially designed to make the most of the iPad's touchscreen interface.

How does the iPad connect to the computer?

The two can communicate via your home wireless network or by using a special USB cable, which is also used for charging your iPad.

Is the onscreen keyboard easy to use?

Apple are very proud of the iPad's touchscreen keyboard and the accompanying error-correcting software that aims to minimize typos. In general, reviewers and owners alike have been pleasantly surprised at how quickly they've got used to it. Inevitably, however, it's not to everyone's taste. When using many applications you can rotate the iPad through ninety degrees to use a bigger version of the keyboard in landscape mode, or even call forth a special split-keyboard option (**Settings > General > Keyboard**).

Of course, with the third-gen iPad also comes the option to dictate rather than use the keyboard (see p.84), and though you will probably need to edit dictated text with the keyboard, it can save you a lot of tapping.

Does the iPad feature handwriting recognition technologies?

No, not straight out of the box. But there are several note-taking apps in the App Store that can handle handwriting recognition … or more likely, fingerwriting recognition. A good example worth looking at is WritePad.

Do I need a computer to use an iPad?

No. Originally iPads could only be activated with a Mac or PC but that isn't true any more thanks to iCloud (see overleaf). However, a computer is still essential for some iPad tasks. For example, if you want to copy a CD onto your iPad, you'll first need to copy it onto a computer with a CD drive. You can, however, download music and video files straight to the iPad from the iTunes Store.

What's iTunes?

iTunes is a piece of software produced by Apple for Macs and PCs. Its main function is as a tool for importing, downloading and managing audio and video. However, iTunes also functions as the hub for selectively moving content from your computer – such as music, video, and photos from your archive – across to your iPad. iTunes can also be used for syncing contacts, calendars and other information with your computer – though these tasks can also be taken care of by iCloud.

What's iCloud?

iCloud is Apple's service for synchronizing content and settings between multiple devices – including iPhones, iPads, iPods and computers. Launched in late 2011, iCloud allows you to ensure, for example, that when you download a song to your iPad it will also appear in iTunes on your Mac, or when you take a photo on your iPad that it will also appear in the photo library on your iPhone. iCloud is free to use, though you have to pay if you require more than five gigabytes of online storage space (not including items purchased from Apple, which are stored for free). See p.58 for more information.

This is the cloud the way it should be: automatic and effortless. iCloud is seamlessly integrated into your apps, so you can access your content on all your devices. And it's free with iOS 5.
Learn more ›

What's MobileMe?

MobileMe was an Apple subscription service that provided a suite of online tools in return for an annual fee – including various tools for iPad users. However, the service was discontinued for new users in 2011, with the launch of iCloud. Existing MobileMe users will have access to some services into 2012, before being fully transitioned to iCloud.

What's an app?

App is short for application – a piece of software designed to fulfil a particular function. If you're used to a PC, an app is basically the same as a program. On the iPad an app might be anything from a game, a word processor or a retro-styled alarm clock, to a version of a popular website with extra features added specially for the iPad.

There are hundreds of thousands of apps available to download from the App Store, some of which have been downloaded and installed on millions of devices.

What apps can I expect to find on my new iPad?

Straight out of the box, the iPad features several apps that will be familiar to anyone who has owned an iPod touch or iPhone. There's Mail, Photos, Notes, Calendar, Contacts, Maps and YouTube (no prizes for guessing what any of those do) and also Safari (Apple's excellent web-browsing application). The iPad also comes with a built-in Music app (for music and other audio content) and a Videos app, for playing back movies, TV shows and other video content. Though familiar, all of these applications have been reworked to make the best use of the iPad's screen size.

Apple have also built several other excellent iPad apps including Remote (see p.178), iBooks (see p.192), iPhoto (see p.146) and Pages (see p.244), from the iWork suite, all of which have to be downloaded separately from the iTunes App Store.

So, the iPad can run iPhone apps?

As already mentioned, the iPhone, iPod touch and the iPad all run versions of the same software, and one of the upshots of this is that pretty much all applications found in the iTunes App Store will run on the iPad. However, it's worth understanding the distinction between apps that are designed to work on both iPads and smaller-screen devices (and present a different interface, depending on the device) and those

that were built for the iPod touch or iPhone and run on the iPad scaled-up to fit nearly all of the screen (pictured) using the iPad's 2x mode.

Scaled apps are not always ideal. Firstly, the graphics can end up looking rather chunky (because each pixel within the app has had its real estate quadrupled), but also, the actual layout of many apps (designed for a pocket-sized device) can seem very odd on the larger screen, leaving you feeling like a diminutive Alice after a sip from the "Drink Me" bottle.

It will be interesting to see how this situation plays out, given the alternatives available to developers. Many developers have already created separate versions of their existing apps for the iPad or created a version that works on both – the latter sometimes referred to as universal apps.

TIP Universal apps, designed to work with a native interface on any iOS device, are denoted by a small + sign next to the price on App Store pages.

So, basically, any app is going to work?

Not necessarily. Keep in mind that some apps popular on the iPhone utilize its cellular call features and that neither first-, second- nor third-gen iPads can be used to make cellular calls. Also remember that if you have a camera-less first-generation iPad, many photo- and video-shooting apps will be about as useful as a chocolate kettle.

How many apps can I load onto the iPad?

As with the iPhone and iPod touch, the iPad can accommodate multiple Home Screens. You can have up to eleven of them, and each holds up to twenty items – either single apps or folders of apps. App folders (see p.71) can hold up to twenty apps each.

The Dock at the bottom of the Home Screen houses another six (the same six across each Home Screen). Which tots up to a massive 4406 potential slots for apps. This number includes both the built-in application icons that you can't remove and any web-clip icons that you might have added (see p.72).

As for data storage capacity, the bigger issue is having enough space (or free time, come to think of it) to fill all 4406 slots, even though many apps are relatively small. To see how much of your iPad's capacity is accounted for, and by which apps, navigate to **Settings** > **General** > **Usage**. Alternatively, connect to iTunes, highlight the device in the sidebar and look at the multicoloured panel at the bottom.

As it's made by Apple, will it also run Mac applications?

No, it's a completely different system that requires applications to be designed with Multi-Touch interactivity in mind. That said, many developers do build separate incarnations of their more popular applications: for example, there may be a version for desktop and laptop Mac machines (sold via the Mac App Store) and an iPad version (for sale in the iTunes App Store).

Connectivity questions

Can I make voice or video phone calls with it?

If you have a second- or third-gen iPad, then yes, video calls are possible thanks to the built-in cameras. Apple's own FaceTime app makes the whole process very straightforward, though both you and your fellow FaceTimers will need to be connected to Wi-Fi for things to work. See p.115 for more.

Other VoIP (Voice over Internet Protocol) services such as Skype have apps available that allow video calls on iPads with cameras. As for voice calls, all iPad models feature a built-in microphone and a single mono speaker (the headphone output jack is stereo), so calls are possible using VoIP services.

Don't be fooled, however, into thinking that you can use either a 4G or 3G iPad as a cellphone: these models do allow you to connect to a phone operator's network, but these connections are for data transfers only (emails, web browsing, etc), not cellular calls or SMS.

Will I be able to get 4G connection speeds with my new iPad?

At the time of writing, probably not. Even though the 2012 iPad is 4G-ready, most countries around the world are yet to roll out 4G network connectivity (see p.23), something for which Apple received considerable flak at the time of the third-generation iPad's launch, given that it was marketed so heavily as a 4G device.

Can you tell me more about the iPad's connectivity?

All iPad models have built-in support for Bluetooth and Wi-Fi. More specifically, they support the current fastest Wi-Fi standard: 802.11n. Wi-Fi standards are backwards compatible, so you should have no

4G, 3G, EDGE and GPRS ... what's all that about?

Over time, the technology used to transmit and receive data using mobile devices has improved, allowing greater range and speed. Of the network technologies widely available at present, 4G (fourth generation) is the most advanced, while 3G (third generation) is currently the most commonly deployed standard. While 3G allows internet access at speeds comparable to basic home broadband connections, say, 2 megabits per second (2 Mbps), 4G can, in theory, deliver anything up to 1 gigabit of data per second (1 Gbps) ... which, needless to say, is pretty fast. That said, there are many networks that label services as 4G or 4G LTE, but that deliver data speeds that are significantly lower than what the 4G standard is capable of. There are many reasons for this, some geographical, some related to network capacity, some based on whether the user is stationary or moving.

Unsurprisingly, it's this speedy 4G standard that the 4G-compatible iPad models use to supply a data connection when there are no Wi-Fi networks available. You'll know you're connected, as "4G" will appear alongside the signal indicator bars on the iPad's Status Bar at the top of the screen. If 4G is not available (and it's worth noting that at the time of writing it isn't in most parts of the world), then the iPad will automatically connect to a 3G signal and display "3G" in the Status Bar. At other times, however, you may see "EDGE" appearing on the Status Bar. EDGE (or Enhanced Data rates for GSM Evolution, to give it its rather grand full name) is a slower standard of data network (sometimes referred to as "2.75G"), which is more widely available in non-urban areas than 4G and 3G. You'll find when connected to EDGE that browsing the web is far slower, but battery life better. EDGE offers a theoretical top speed of 236 kilobits per second (kbps); in practice, however, users have more often than not experienced data rates as slow as 50 kbps – like an old-fashioned dial-up connection.

Slower still is the GPRS standard, which is represented by a ° icon on the iPad's Status Bar.

issues connecting to Wi-Fi networks that support the older 802.11b and 802.11g standards, although early iPad adopters did run into these exact problems during the first few weeks of the iPad's release back in

2010. Unless you encounter any specific issues with a particular home network setup, there really is no need to worry about all these different standards, as they can generally all coexist happily.

The cellular-capable versions of the iPad include a SIM card tray, which houses a special cell network SIM card. 4G and 3G are data standards used by many cellphone network providers to handle the ever-growing data demands of their customers. If you suspect that you are largely going to use your iPad at home and connect via Wi-Fi, you may well not need the option of a 4G/3G connection. If, however, you are looking to employ your iPad in the wider world – on the commute to work, say – then it's well worth considering.

Can I "unlock" the iPad and use my current cellphone's SIM card and network?

When the iPhone was first launched, each purchased device was "locked" to a specific network. Naturally, it didn't take geeks long to figure out how to "unlock" the iPhone's software for use with any SIM card and network.

So, to answer your question with regard to the iPad: there's some good news and some bad. The good news is that in the majority of territories cellular-capable iPads come officially unlocked, which means that you can choose which network provider you want to go with, without having to worry about invalidating your warranty or messing with the software.

But before you go and crack open your cellphone to get at the SIM, here's the bad news. The iPad uses a special Micro-SIM card (also known as a 3FF SIM), so the one you currently use won't fit. What's more, there aren't that many network providers yet offering the Micro-SIM, which will, at least for a while, seriously limit your choice of network.

The bad news for US customers is that the iPad comes locked to either Verizon or AT&T, both of which use different network standards and different SIMs, making the possibility of switching network very hard.

Do I need to worry about different types of cellular network? GSM, UMTS, etc?

GSM and UMTS are both flavours of 3G technology, and there are also numerous technology flavours of 4G appearing around the world (namely HSPA, HSPA+ and DC-HSDPA). Though you really don't need to know what all this means, in some countries you do need to purchase your device tailored to a specific data network provider (basically, the hardware is the same, but the firmware is different). As already stated, in the US example, the choice is between AT&T and Verizon, and you make your selection when purchasing. As you can imagine, this distinction has made the secondhand market, particularly, a minefield.

What are APN settings?

APN stands for Access Point Name (you never know, it might come up in a crossword one day). Found within **Settings > Cellular Data > APN Settings**, these special configurations are used by your iPad to connect to your cellular data network provider. You should never have to give them a second thought as they are automatically set up by your SIM card, though if you do ever find yourself with cellular network connectivity issues, it's worth verifying with your provider that they are right.

Can my iPad be tethered to my iPhone?

Tethering is the process whereby one device connects to the internet via the online connection of another device. If you have an iPhone 4 or 4S, you can set up its Personal Hotspot feature to allow your iPad to connect via Bluetooth or Wi-Fi and take advantage of your iPhone's cellular connectivity – very handy if you have a Wi-Fi-only iPad.

If you have a 4G iPad, and your network provider supports the service, you can also enable your tablet as a personal Wi-Fi hotspot (maybe for getting a laptop online).Whichever device you are using to create a Personal Hotspot, expect to end up paying over and above your regular data tariff for the privilege of doing so.

Can I use the iPad overseas?

When it comes to foreign use of web, email, maps and other internet-based features, you're best sticking to Wi-Fi hotspots where you can get online for free (or pay a reasonable charge for access). In many countries it's possible to connect via the local cellular phone networks if you have a 3G or 4G iPad, but be prepared for some really savage fees. If you can stomach the costs, turn Data Roaming on within **Settings > Cellular Data**. Perhaps the best solution is to purchase a compatible 3G data SIM locally when you go abroad and then access the data networks at the local rate.

Does the iPad feature a GPS system?

4G and 3G models include an actual GPS (Global Positioning System) chip. Similar to the iPhone, this offers so-called "Assisted GPS", which means it combines satellite positioning data with cellular network data (a triangulation of the nearest network masts) and also any available Wi-Fi network data. The Wi-Fi-only model docs not contain a GPS chip, so relies on connected Wi-Fi networks to determine its position.

And what about a compass?

All iPad models include a built-in digital compass, which allows the built-in Maps app and hundreds of other navigation apps to help the iPad point you in the right direction.

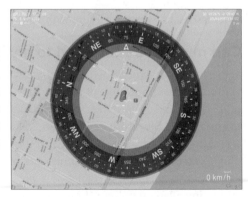

Though you can use the digital compass on the iPad to navigate within the built-in Maps app, there are also many other apps that add a bit more spice to the experience. The free Commander Compass Lite is a good case in point.

Will these "location services" work overseas without costing me a fortune in roaming charges?

It's worth noting that the digital compass and location-aware features *can* operate independently of data roaming. So, as long as you use an app with "offline" mapping features (i.e., the map data is downloaded as part of the app, and not pulled from the internet as and when it is needed), you should be able to get a fix on your current location using a 4G or 3G iPad with roaming turned off.

iPad vs Macs and PCs

Should I go for a tablet or a netbook?

The iPad can't run the same versions of the applications you use on a PC, and it doesn't have a conventional file and folder system like Windows does. Standard input and output ports, such as USB and LAN, are also missing, as is a CD/DVD drive. Critics routinely point out that the iPad does not support Adobe's Flash media format, which is required to view content on many popular websites. Finally, it's worth noting that you will pay a premium (often referred to as the "Apple Tax") for the quality and design of Apple products.

All that said, netbooks and other diminutive laptops also have their issues, the two killers being the frustratingly small keyboards and screens, and the fact that they often don't boast the processing power they should to deal with fully fledged operating systems. The end result is frequently a slow and clunky experience.

As for the choice between the iPad and a netbook, it's down to personal preference. Note, however, that when Steve Jobs (Apple's then CEO) unveiled the iPad in 2010 he specifically stated that netbooks are "not better than laptops at anything, they're just cheaper". Perhaps unsurprisingly, the popularity of netbooks has significantly dropped off in the two years that tablets, such as the iPad, have been around.

So what about the other tablet choices?

There are dozens of alternatives to choose from, including many running Google's Android OS, the best of which, arguably, have come from Samsung in their Galaxy range. The Kindle Fire and Nook, meanwhile, are great eBook readers, but not as powerful as the iPad. And if it is a range of apps and a decent ecosystem for consuming music and video that you are interested in, the iPad will undoubtedly be your best choice.

Can the iPad download music and video directly from the iTunes Store?

Yes, absolutely, and it is the only tablet that can access the iTunes Store. You will, however, need to be connected to a Wi-Fi or cellular data network to get online and access the store. Once the files have downloaded you can watch or listen straight away and, thanks to iCloud, anything you download will also automatically make its way onto your Mac or PC, along with any other Apple devices you might own.

Will the iPad replace my Mac or PC at home?

Good question. The short answer is yes, it might. However, even if it fulfils all your domestic needs (email, web browsing, eBook reading, say), you may still want to connect it to a Mac or PC so that it can synchronize with your iTunes library via a USB connection or Wi-Fi, or perhaps import music that you only have on CD. You might also have an extensive photo library on your Mac or PC and want to sync albums to your iPad.

Everything else that was traditionally managed by iTunes (backups, software updates, video and music syncing, contacts, calendars and bookmarks syncing) can now all be managed by the aforementioned iCloud service (see p.58).

The most compelling reason to hold onto your desktop Mac or PC at home is capacity, as iPads are still relatively slight compared to many modern computers which may have terabytes of storage space available.

Is my current computer up to the job?

If you do want to sync via iTunes, and you bought a PC or Mac in the last few years, it will probably be capable of running the desired version of iTunes (version 10.6 or later). If you don't already have iTunes installed, it can be downloaded for free from Apple's website: itunes.com.

As far as the operating system is concerned, you must have either a Mac running Mac OS X 10.5.8 or later (if you are still using Tiger, it's time to upgrade), or a Windows PC running Windows Vista, Windows 7 or Windows XP (SP3). To see the latest on compatible system requirements for iPad syncing, visit: apple.com/ipad/specs.

> **TIP** For advice on when to upgrade your Mac computer in relation to Apple's current product cycles, visit macrumors.com.

How is the iPad for web browsing and email?

Though few pocket-sized internet devices can match a computer with large screen, mouse and a full-sized keyboard, the iPad does an excellent job of providing the functionality and speed of a full-sized machine, but with the intuitive touchscreen interface of the iPad. Tabbed web browsing is especially well handled, with a great interface for zooming in and out on sections of a webpage and a really handy thumbnail view for moving between pages.

The email tool is impressive too – the app's split-column view in landscape mode is particularly pleasing to use.

Can it edit Word and Excel docs?

The iPad can automatically open, read and forward Word, Excel and PowerPoint docs sent by email or found online. However, to edit them you will need to download a separate app – search the App Store to see what's currently available. Also, check out Apple's own iWork apps: Pages (which can edit Word docs), Numbers (which can work with Excel docs) and Keynote (which handles PowerPoint docs).

Can I use an iPad as a hard drive to move files between computers?

Unlike the iPod, the iPad doesn't offer a "disk mode" to allow storage and transfer of any types of computer files. However, there are many third-party apps (such as Air Sharing and iFiles) that allow you to sync files between a computer and an iPad via Wi-Fi.

There are also many apps (including those within the iWork suite) that allow you to move files on and off the iPad via the Apps panel (pictured below) within iTunes when an iPad is connected.

Even better, sign up with a service such as Dropbox and take your storage and syncing online. The excellent Dropbox app can be used to view many of your stored files on the iPad.

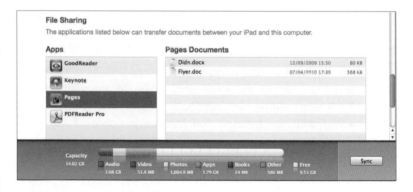

Can I use the iPad as a touch-sensitive control pad for my Mac or PC?

Though Apple don't include that kind of functionality straight out of the box, there are numerous applications in the App Store that will let you use the iPad in the same way you might the touch-pad on a laptop. Air Mouse and TouchPad are both worth a look, though the bigger challenge might be trying to keep the iPad still and stable whilst lying on its back on your desk. A few lumps of Blu-Tack work a treat.

eBooks and iBooks

Isn't "iBook" the name of an Apple laptop?

You're not wrong. The iBook *was* an Apple laptop, produced under various guises between 1999 and 2006, when it disappeared to be superseded by the MacBook. Whether the shift in naming conventions had anything to do with a long-term road map that included the development of an eBook store is unknown, but the term is back, and now refers to iBooks, the iPad's eBook reader app, which also acts as a doorway to Apple's iBookstore. The store features content from several major publishers, including HarperCollins and Penguin, as well as a vast library of free-to-read out-of-copyright classic titles courtesy of Project Gutenberg. The iBookstore makes its prose titles available in the popular ePub eBook format, which is ideally suited for flowing text; the

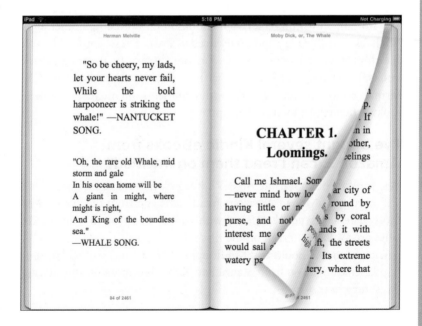

iBookstore also accommodates various special, or "enhanced" books that might incorporate video, audio, and interactive "widgets", that in some instances can be almost app-like.

As well as being able to handle titles downloaded from the iBookstore, the iBooks app can display titles from other stores, assuming they peddle their books as DRM-free ePubs. For more on all this, turn to p.192.

What's DRM?

DRM (digital rights management) is the practice of embedding special code in audio, video or eBook files to limit what the user can do with those files. For example, ePub titles downloaded from the iBookstore are only readable within the iBooks app.

Can I read PDF documents on the iPad?

PDFs can be opened and read via web links from Safari and from Mail when sent to the iPad as an attachment. You can then choose to view and store them within either your iBooks library or certain other apps (such as GoodReader and PDF Reader Pro). These apps add both file storage and document reader functionality to the iPad – great for books, magazines and journals that have been made available in PDF format. As for annotating PDFs with comments, highlights, etc, take a look at the neu.Annotate+ PDF app.

I've bought several Kindle eBooks from Amazon ... can I read them on my iPad?

Yes, you can, but not using Apple's homegrown iBooks app; instead you will need to download Amazon's free Kindle app from the iTunes App Store. The app syncs seamlessly with Amazon so that all your Kindle titles are available to read on the iPad.

Aside from the iBooks and Kindle apps, there are many other "reader" apps including those from Stanza and Kobo. For more on the alternatives, turn to p.203.

Getting technical

What kind of display does the iPad have?

The iPad's screen is glass, with a so-called "oleophobic" coating, first used by Apple on the iPhone 3GS, which makes it far easier to banish greasy smudges and finger marks compared to the screens on earlier iPhone models. The finish on the screen is glossy, which may not be to some people's taste; overall, however, the LED backlighting of the display is bright enough to outweigh any issues caused by reflections.

The iPad uses a liquid crystal display (or LCD), more specifically the in-plane switching (IPS) variety. These are incredibly high-quality screens that allow for a wide angle of view without any significant shift in colour or deterioration of the image. The so-called "Retina display" of the third-gen iPad gives an incredibly sharp and vivid image – better than you might find on many regular computer screens.

The Apple A4 & A5 chips

Having previously always purchased their microchips from third-party manu-facturers, a few years back Apple took the rather bold step of shelling out $300 million for a California-based computer processor development company called PA Semi, so that they could design and manufacture their own. The end result, without going into too many of the techie details, was the in-house development of the "Apple A4" chip and its so-called "system on a chip" (or SOC) design. The SOC design integrates the main processor with the graphics processor, the memory controller and some other odds and ends that would normally exist outside the processor unit. The result is fast and energy efficient (leading to a longer battery life).

The 1GHz A4 processor ended up under the hood of the first-generation iPads. The second-gen iPad sported the even faster dual-core A5, while the current third-gen model boasts the even swifter A5X chip and quad-core graphics, dramatically improving the device's speed and performance over those of its predecessors.

Is the backlighting hard on the eyes?

As with using any computing device with a colour backlit screen, eye strain can be an issue. However, the potential for eye strain is outweighed by the multi-functional nature of the device, the colour screen and the overall build quality of the iPad, when compared to single-function eBook readers such as the E Ink Amazon Kindles.

As for eye strain, the best advice is simply to be aware of the issue and find your own comfort level of screen brightness and time spent reading. Take regular breaks and allow your eyes to refocus on distant objects. It's all common sense, really.

What is the back made from?

The back of the iPad is crafted from a single piece of aluminium, with a satin matt finish. It is similar in feel to the shells of Apple's "unibody" MacBook Air and MacBook Pro laptops.

Does the iPad contain a hard drive?

No. Like the MacBook Air, modern iPods, and also the iPhone, the iPad stores its information on so-called flash memory: tiny chips of the kind found in digital camera memory cards and flash drives. These have a smaller capacity than hard drives, but they're less bulky, less power-hungry and less likely to break if the device is dropped.

If I buy a 16GB or 32GB model, can I add more internal storage later?

No. What you get is what you get.

Does it have built-in stereo speakers?

No, the iPad has only the one speaker, which is mono and situated on its lower edge near the Dock connector. It's also worth mentioning that this speaker is surprisingly loud and sounds really pretty good.

The headphone jack, which is located on the iPad's top edge is, however, stereo, and can be used to connect the iPad to an external speaker system. Equally, an Apple iPad Dock features a dedicated stereo line-out socket for connecting to external speaker systems.

And a microphone?

The microphone (which you will most likely use for either video calls or dictation) can be found in the form of a tiny hole at the top of the iPad's rear casing. So that's where you need to aim at when talking.

And should I expect great things from the cameras?

The rear-facing camera on the third-gen iPad delivers 5-megapixel photos and HD video (1080p) captured at up to 30 frames per second, which is more than good enough for most purposes. The front-facing camera is primarily designed for FaceTime video calling and can only deliver VGA-quality images and video.

Battery questions

Does it take AAs?

No … the iPad comes with an integrated, inaccessible, rechargeable lithium ion battery, which, according to Apple, will give you "up to 10 hours" of surfing the web over a Wi-Fi connection, and "9 hours" over a mobile data network. The battery is recharged via the Dock connector port on the iPad's lower edge when connected using a USB cable to either a computer (Mac or PC) or an Apple power adapter (one of these is included in the box with the iPad). It can also be charged from either of these sources via an Apple iPad Dock.

There are also many third-party docking solutions that can be used to charge a connected iPad, though older peripherals are often not compatible, even though the Dock connector might physically connect.

So what do I do if the battery dies? Can I replace it?

Like those of iPods and iPhones, the iPad's battery gradually dies over time and can only be replaced by Apple for a substantial fee (in the US, the cost is $105.95 including shipping). This lack of user access to the battery is a state of affairs for which Apple have had quite a bit of bad publicity over the years.

To be fair, however, all rechargeable batteries deteriorate over time and eventually die. The high cost of the Apple replacement process can partly be explained by the nature of the device. The power requirements of an iPad are comparable to that of a laptop – and laptop batteries are even more expensive. As for sending the device back to Apple, this is irritating, though it reflects the fact that the device has a properly sealed design and is thus free from the flimsy battery flaps that often get broken on similar non-Apple hardware.

I heard that Apple will actually replace the whole iPad if the battery dies. Is this true?

Yes, this is true. For the money you hand over, you'll actually get a replacement iPad. This new iPad will not contain any of the data or content that was on the device that you sent to Apple, so it is essential that you make a backup (see p.258) of the content to either iCloud or iTunes before you mail it off. For security reasons, you might also want to wipe all your content before heading to the post office, just in case the device goes astray.

Does the Apple warranty cover battery replacement?

The standard Apple warranty will only cover battery replacement for free if the battery turns out to be defective during the period of the warranty. If that happens, and your device is registered with Apple, your best bet is to head straight to a bricks and mortar Apple Store, where they may well be able to give you a replacement device there and then. At the time of writing, however, if you purchase the two-year AppleCare cover, then Apple will replace the battery if its capacity drops below fifty percent of its original capacity. Be sure to check the terms and conditions of the AppleCare policy before you sign up, as these details may differ depending on the territory in which you live. For more on iPad batteries, looking after them, and replacements, turn to p.260.

Internet questions

Does the iPad offer fast internet access?

That depends where you are and the kind of iPad you have. If you're within range of a Wi-Fi network, as found in homes, offices, cafés (and across some entire cities), then your internet access will typically be pretty speedy: not quite as fast as with a top-end Mac or PC, but not a long way off.

If, on the other hand, you're out and about, away from any accessible Wi-Fi networks – walking down the street, say, or sitting on a bus – then you will need an iPad with 4G or 3G capabilities to stand a chance of getting connected.

In this instance you will be connecting via a mobile phone network and the connection will probably not be as impressive as that experienced over most Wi-Fi networks, but it will be good enough. (For more on the various flavours of cell network connection, see the box on p.23.)

Another factor worth knowing about when out and about is, believe it or not, your own speed of travel. If you are travelling on a train or in a moving car, you might find that your connection speed becomes slower than when you are stationary. This is because the device is having to accommodate a constantly shifting relationship to the nearby signal masts that it's connecting with, making it hard for the iPad to maintain a constant and coherent stream of data to and from the internet.

Will all websites work on an iPad?

The iPad features a fully fledged web browser – Safari – which will work with the overwhelming majority of websites. The main catch is that certain special types of web content won't display:

• **Flash animations** Widely used for banner ads (no great loss there), interactive graphics and a few entire websites.

• **Java applications** Not to be confused with JavaScript (which works fine on an iPad), Java is used for certain online programs such as calendar tools or broadband speed tests.

• **Some music and video** Music and video clips will usually work fine, assuming you have a reasonable connection – though quite a few are encoded using Flash. These ones won't show up.

Can you tell me more about Safari?

The iPad's Safari web browser is a streamlined version of the browser shipped on all Macs, and a similar version can also be found on both iPhones and the iPod touch. Apple also have a PC version available.

The version on the iPad supports features such as tabbed browsing, private browsing and a very useful Reader mode: great for news and longer articles. There are also loads of alternative browser apps to be found in the App Store if Safari is not to your taste.

Does the iPad synchronize bookmarks with my computer?

Yes. It works with Safari on Macs, and Safari or Internet Explorer on PCs, and syncing of bookmarks can be achieved either via iCloud or via iTunes. Firefox isn't currently supported, though the excellent, and free, Xmarks service can be used to unify bookmarks between all your computer browsers. Find out more from xmarks.com.

Will the iPad work with my email account?

For a personal email account, almost certainly. The iPad is compatible with all standard email technologies, such as POP3 and IMAP, and ships preset to work with AOL, Yahoo!, Microsoft Exchange, iCloud, MobileMe and Gmail (aka Google Mail). If you use Outlook on a PC or Mail on a Mac, the iPad will even sync your account details across from your desktop machine, so you don't have to set anything up.

The only time you're likely to encounter problems is when setting up a work email account. This may or may not be possible, depending on the policies of your network administrators.

Does the iPad present any security risks?

Not really. There's a theoretical risk with any device capable of connecting to Wi-Fi networks that someone could "hack" it remotely and access any stored information. But the risk is extremely small. The main risk – as with any phone or laptop – is that someone could steal it and access private data. If you're worried about that possibility, the best defence is to password-protect your iPad's screen – look within **Settings > General > Passcode Lock**.

Should I let my children use it to get online?

The iPad doesn't pose any significantly different risks to those of other types of computer that your children might use to get online, and there are measures that you can take to make sure that your children stay safe. Under **Settings > General > Restrictions**, set access options for iTunes content and also determine whether other users may download some kinds of content at all. You can also block access to YouTube and Safari completely if you wish.

Because, at the time of writing, the iPad does not support different user accounts for different members of the family, all these settings can be a bit of a hassle; be sure also to talk to your kids about online safety so that they can develop their own online security skills.

Oh, and while I think of it...

Will the iPad work with my old iPhone and iPod accessories?

Maybe. The Dock socket on the bottom of the iPad is the same as those on recent iPods and iPhones, so accessories should be able to connect. That doesn't necessarily mean they'll work, however. At the time of writing, the success rate seems to be around fifty–fifty, as many older devices don't support the newer operating system that runs on the iPad.

Does it have Voice Command or Siri, like recent iPhone models do?

No, unfortunately it doesn't, though you can dictate text whenever you see the microphone icon to the left of the space bar on the keyboard. You might want to try a voice-triggered search app such as Evi as an interim solution.

Is the iPad good for games?

Yes, absolutely … there's an ever-expanding category within the App Store dedicated to gaming apps. Add to this Games Center (Apple's online social gaming network) and the ability to mirror your screen activity to a TV or projector (via either an Apple TV or an iPad to HDMI cable; see p.185) and you have a pretty compelling gaming platform that can do almost anything that a traditional gaming console can.

For reviews of all the newest and coolest games, visit slidetoplay.com and toucharcade.com.

Okay, I'm sold on the idea; where can I get one?

Read on, and all will be revealed.

02

Buying options

Which model? Where from?

At the time of going to press there are four hardware decisions you need to make: whether you want a second- or third-generation device, how much storage space you need your iPad to have, what sort of connectivity you want to go for (Wi-Fi or Wi-Fi and mobile data connectivity) and, most importantly, whether you want it in white or black. The second-generation iPad only comes in the 16GB size, and is very much the budget entry choice, while the third-gen device has three sizes on offer. In this chapter we'll take a look at the specific choices (focusing largely on the third-generation iPad) and also touch upon various other buying options you might want to think about.

How many gigs do you need?

Choosing how much storage capacity to go for is one of the trickier decisions. Remember that you don't necessarily need an iPad capable of holding your entire music or video collection. You can store your full collection on your computer's hard drive and just copy across to your iPad the songs or albums you want to listen to at any one time. The same goes for your photo collection – you don't need to keep it all on both your iPad and regular computer.

True storage capacity

The first thing you should know is that your iPad may offer slightly less space than you expect. All computer storage devices are in reality about 7 percent smaller than advertised because hardware manufacturers use gigabyte to mean one billion bytes, whereas in computing reality it should be 230, which equals 1.0737 billion bytes. This is a bit of a scam, but everyone does it and no one wants to break the mould.

Moreover, a few hundred megabytes of the remaining 93 percent of space is used to store the iPad's operating system, applications and firmware. All told, then, you can expect to lose a decent chunk of space before you load a single video, song or app to your new device. The following table refers to the difference between advertised capacity and actual capacity for the third-generation iPad, launched in March 2012:

Advertised capacity	Real capacity	Actual free space
64GB	59.6GB	58.1GB
32GB	29.8GB	27.9GB
16GB	14.9GB	13.3GB

To see the actual free space figure on your iPad, look for it under **Capacity** within **Settings > General > About**.

How big is a gig?

A gigabyte (GB) is, roughly speaking, the same as a thousand megabytes (MB) or a million kilobytes (KB). Here are some examples of what you can fit in each gigabyte.

		1GB =
Music	at 128 kbps (medium quality)	250 typical tracks
	at 256 kbps (high quality)	125 typical tracks
	at 992 kbps (CD quality)	35 typical tracks
Audiobooks	at 32 kbps	70 hours
Photos	5 Megapixel images	525 photos
Movies SD	a 90-minute standard movie	0.75 movies
Movies HD	a 90-minute HD movie	0.25 movies

Checking your current data needs

If you already use iTunes to store music and video, then you can easily get an idea of how much space your existing collection takes up. In the left-hand sidebar, click **Music**, **Movies**, **Podcasts** or any playlist and the bottom of the iTunes window will reveal the total disk space that the selected item occupies (as pictured below).

As for photographs, the size of the images on your computer and the amount of space they occupy there bears little relation to the space the same images will take up on an iPad. This is because when iTunes copies photos to your iPad, it resizes them for use on the device's screen.

9	✔	Last Call	4:34	Elliott Smith	Roman Candle
10	✔	Cactus	2:17	Pixies	Surfer Rosa
11	✔	Taste of Cindy (Acoustic)	2:02	The Jesus & Mary Chain	Barbed Wire Kisses
12	✔	Werewolf	4:05	Cat Power	You Are Free
13	✔	Colours	2:57	Peter Moyse	Peter Moyse EP
14	✔	I Wish I Knew	3:45	Sharon Van Etten	Sharon Van Etten
15	✔	Hunted by A Freak	4:18	Mogwai	Happy Songs For Happ
16	✔	06 Codex	4:47	Radiohead	King Of Limbs

23 songs, 1:24:52 total time, 222.2 MB

What are the options?

At the time of writing, there are three storage sizes available: 16GB, 32GB and 64GB. At the 16GB level you have the choice between the iPad 2, and the higher-powered third-gen model.

Interestingly, during the run-up to the US launch of the iPad 2, pre-orders through the Apple website favoured the lowest-capacity device by almost two-to-one over the highest-capacity version, perhaps suggesting that early adopters saw its use as primarily a web browsing or email device, and not somewhere to store loads of content. This is worth thinking about, as you might not need as much capacity as you think, especially if you intend to use the iPad at home. That said, if you plan to get creative with your iPad, editing video or music, or working with photos, then you are going to fill a 16GB device pretty quickly … and you can't add extra storage later.

TIP For the latest iPad tech specs and prices, visit the Apple website: apple.com/ipad.

Wi-Fi or Wi-Fi+4G?

There is also the connectivity question to be addressed. If you only intend to use the iPad at home, and have a wireless network up and running, then go for the Wi-Fi-only model; if you intend to take the thing out and about, then there is a strong case for going for the Wi-Fi+4G version. In the latter case, you are going to need a SIM card and to sign up for a mobile data service plan. In many countries, you can get hold of a free Micro-SIM card from the Apple Store when you buy your iPad; if not, you'll have to get one direct from a network provider. The Apple site is the best place to compare the available tariffs and deals. Visit apple.com/ipad/4g and click on the flag, bottom right, to find your country's page.

Tethering

As already mentioned (p.25), it is possible to use an iPhone 4 or 4S (as well as many non-Apple smartphones) to create your own personal Wi-Fi hotspot and "tether" your iPad to it. For many this will be a fantastic way to get a Wi-Fi-only iPad online, avoiding the need to pay extra for an iPad with data network connectivity. But before you completely disregard the 3G or 4G iPad option, it is worth remembering the following. The Wi-Fi-only model does not include the more accurate GPS chip of the 3G and 4G iPads; tethering can be a bit of a pain if you are having to constantly mess about with multiple devices; you may well need a special data plan on your phone that allows tethering; and, finally, your phone will run out of juice quicker if it has to pump out a Wi-Fi signal.

The nature of the service plans varies slightly from territory to territory, though all have roughly the same setup. In the US, for example, both AT&T and Verizon offer three options:

Data provider	Monthly data	Cost
AT&T	**250MB per month**	**$14.99**
AT&T	**3GB per month**	**$30.00**
AT&T	**5GB per month**	**$50.00**
Verizon	**1GB per month**	**$20.00**
Verizon	**2GB per month**	**$30.00**
Verizon	**5GB per month**	**$50.00**

All of these deals are prepaid a month in advance, and there is no lengthy contract, which means that you might only set it up every now and again, and for only a month at a time, perhaps when heading out of town on a trip. Also expect to have thrown in Wi-Fi usage via any hotspot networks that the carrier might have in place.

In many territories (but not the US) you can go with any cellular provider, as long as they can supply you with a compatible Micro-SIM card and a suitable tariff.

Most importantly, however, it is worth trying to ascertain the coverage provided by the various companies you are choosing between as, particularly in the US, there are some pretty significant areas that may or may not get coverage from particular providers.

What about data roaming?

Your domestic data plan is unlikely to include data roaming (using cellular data networks to access the web, send emails, use the Maps app, etc, when abroad). Check what local plans are available in the country you're intending to visit (look on their local Apple website) as the cheapest option is likely to be buying a pre-paid Micro-SIM to put into your iPad when you reach your destination. There are also third parties offering Micro-SIM roaming packs. If you're travelling to Europe, check out maxroam.com.

Where to buy

As with all Apple products, iPads cost basically the same amount no matter where you buy them. The price you'll get direct from Apple will typically be only a few pounds/dollars more (or occasionally less) than the price you'll find from the many other dealers that sell online or on the high street.

Apple Store UK apple.com/ukstore
Apple Store US apple.com/store

That said, different sellers may throw in different extras, such as a case or dock, to get your attention. In the US market a good place to start is the iMore "2012 iPad Buyers' Guides":

iMore imore.com/guides/

Or try a price-comparison agent such as, in the US:

Google Shopping Search google.com/shopping
PriceWatch pricewatch.com
Shopper.com shopper.com

In the UK, price-comparison agents include:

Kelkoo kelkoo.co.uk
Shopping.com uk.shopping.com

Buying from a high-street store typically means paying the full standard price, but you'll get the iPad immediately. If you order over the phone or internet from Apple, you can expect around a week's wait for delivery. For a list of dealers in the UK, follow the link from apple.com/uk/hardware.

In many US and UK cities, you can also go straight to one of Apple's own retail stores, such as the iconic New York City Fifth Avenue branch, pictured here. For a list of all Apple stores, see:

Apple Stores
apple.com/retail

Apple's prestigious flagship store on Fifth Avenue in New York City.

Buying accessories

There's an awful lot of choice out there when it comes to buying accessories for your iPad; and there's also a lot of confusion about which older iPhone and iPod accessories will work with the iPad. As a general rule, assume that any device that came out before 2009 and connects via the Dock Connector isn't going to work. As for what *does* work, Apple produce a handful of items, but there's lots more besides.

You'll almost certainly want to get a case or cover as soon as possible. Some of these resemble all-encompassing leather folio cases (Moleskine make an excellent one) which protect both the iPad's front and back. Others (such as Apple's own Smart Cover, pictured on p.12, for the second- and third-gen models) attach magnetically and feature a flap that, like a book cover, opens to reveal the iPad's screen. Though the back of the iPad remains exposed, its aluminium shell is generally durable enough to deal with everyday bumps and scratches. Whatever you get, be sure that it is versatile enough to act as a stand for both comfortable typing and for watching video.

If you don't get on with the iPad's onscreen keyboard (see p.78) then you might want to invest in a regular Apple Wireless Keyboard, which connects to the iPad via Bluetooth. Most other brands of Bluetooth keyboard will also work, though check with the manufacturer before you buy one. To connect a USB keyboard, try using the Apple Camera Connection Kit as intermediary. To set up a Bluetooth keyboard with the iPad, make sure the peripheral is turned on and has pairing enabled. Then, on the iPad, tap **Settings** > **General** > **Bluetooth**, toggle Bluetooth on and then wait for the device to appear in the list. To unpair, tap the ⊙ icon next to its name and then **Forget This Device**.

As for finding iPad accessories, all Apple Store (store.apple.com) pages feature customer reviews, which can be an invaluable source of information, even if you don't end up buying the goods from Apple. Here are a few review and tech sites that are also worth looking at when choosing iPad extras:

Engadget engadget.com
Slash Gear slashgear.com
Obama Pacman obamapacman.com

For details on adapters to connect your iPad to a TV or projector, turn to p.185.

However, some online retailers tend to be quite quick to deliver, including the best-known of all:

Amazon US amazon.com
Amazon UK amazon.co.uk

Warranties and insurance

If you buy through either the Apple online store or in a bricks-and-mortar Apple Store, then expect to get offered the AppleCare Protection Plan. For $99 (US) you will get two years of cover from the date of purchase instead of the standard one year that you get for free. This covers defects and failures that have not been caused by "damage or abuse". It also covers the replacement of the iPad if its battery capacity drops to less than fifty percent of its original capacity. This price will also give you unlimited telephone technical support for the period of the warranty. Double-check the terms and conditions in your territory, as they might be different to those described above.

It might also be worth investigating the possibility of adding the iPad to your home contents insurance, as this can sometimes include certain items when taken with you outside of the home. Equally, some insurers offer special insurance packages for high-value electronic devices.

Used iPads

Refurbished iPads

Apple and a few other retailers offer refurbished iPads. These will either be end-of-line models or up-to-date ones that have been returned for some reason. They come "as new" – checked, repackaged and with a full standard warranty – but they are reduced in price by up to forty percent (usually more like fifteen percent).

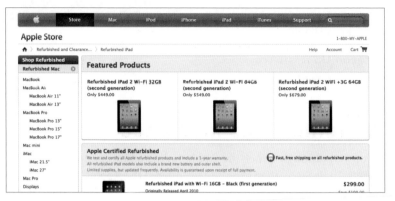

The only problem is availability: the products are in such hot demand that you need to check in regularly in order to see the real bargains, and when you do spot something you want, you shouldn't waste much time in mulling it over, as it will probably go to someone else if you decide to sleep on it.

On the UK and US sites, follow the Special Deals links from apple.com/ukstore and apple.com/store respectively; and in the US, for the most up-to-date information about availability, call 1-800/MY-APPLE. Alternatively, check with your local Apple retailer to see whether they offer refurbished or returned iPads.

Secondhand iPads

Buying a secondhand iPad is much like buying any other piece of used electronic equipment: you might find a bargain but you might land yourself with an overpriced table mat. If you buy one that is less than a year old, it will still be within warranty, so you should be able to get it repaired for free if anything goes wrong inside – even if the iPad in question was purchased in a different country.

Whatever you buy, It's good to see it in action before parting with any cash, but remember that this won't tell you everything. If an iPad's been used a lot, for example, the battery might be on its last legs and soon need replacing, which will add substantially to the cost.

If possible, see if you can negotiate a couple of days with the device before you hand over the cash ... that way you can see how well it holds its charge during use.

If you're looking to buy an iPad with either 3G or 4G connectivity, be sure that you understand the situation in your country regarding whether or not the device will work with multiple carriers. If you aren't sure, play it safe and look to buy one that you know has already been used on the network you want to use.

If you buy on eBay (the excellent eBay app is pictured above), you'll get loads of choice and a certain level of protection against being sold a dud. But be sure to read the auction listing carefully and ask the seller questions if you're unsure of anything.

To buy or to wait?

When shopping for any piece of computer equipment, there's always the tricky question of whether to buy the current model, which may have been around for a few months, or hang on for the next version, which may be better *and* less expensive. In the case of iPads, the situation is even worse, because Apple are famously secretive about their plans to release new or upgraded versions of their hardware.

Unless you have a friend who works in Apple HQ – and an opportunity to get them drunk – you're unlikely to hear anything from the horse's mouth about new iPad models until the day they appear. So, unless a new model came out recently, there's always the possibility that your new purchase will be out of date within a few weeks. The best you can do is check out some sites where rumours of new models are discussed. But don't believe everything you read…

Apple Insider appleinsider.com

Mac Rumors macrumors.com

Recycling your old iPad

You should never throw old electrical equipment in the bin. Not only will it contain chemicals that can be harmful to the environment when incinerated or sent to landfill, it will also contain metals and other materials that can be recycled and used again.

Anyhow, there are plenty of better options. Various groups will take old tablets off your hands – even if they're broken. Apple provide addressed, postage-paid envelopes expressly for the purpose. To order one, visit:

Apple Recycling (US) apple.com/recycling

Apple Recycling (UK) apple.com/uk/recycling

Best of all, Apple will in most cases pay you for your old Apple devices. In the UK you get hard cash, paid straight to your bank account, in the US they dish out Apple Gift Cards.

Getting started

03

The basics

Setup, charging, syncing

It's simple to get started with a new iPad. This chapter covers all the basics – and also provides advice on synchronizing your iPad with iTunes and other devices.

Since late 2011 and the launch of iOS 5, setting up a new iPad is as simple as turning it on and following a few simple instructions. However, if you don't already have an Apple ID (which is basically an email address and password you use for logging into various Apple services and stores), you'll need to set one up as part of the process. You can skip this step if you like, but an Apple ID *is* required for downloading apps and music – and for using iCloud.

Follow the prompts and either create a new Apple email address (see p.60) or use an existing email address as your Apple ID … the latter is the best option as you aren't going to forget an address that you probably already refer to on a daily basis.

The only other thing you may need to know at the outset is how to import all your information and apps from your old iPad. To do this, first sync your old iPad with either iTunes or iCloud (see p.58); then, during the setup process for your new iPad, choose **Restore From Backup** and follow the prompts.

Once the new iPad has restored from the backup and restarted, it then has to go through the lengthy process of checking in with the App Store to redownload all the apps you had installed on the old iPad.

TIP If you have an iPad with Wi-Fi and either 3G or 4G connectivity, you may well also be prompted to sign up for a data plan. For more on this take a look at the Connecting chapter.

Cables and charging

The iPad comes with a USB charge/sync cable. One end attaches to the iPad (either directly or via a Dock), the other end connects to any USB port – on a Mac, PC, USB hub or the supplied 10 watt power adapter (the latter giving you the fastest charge). If you have a 5 watt plug from a recent iPod or iPhone, this will also work, but will charge more slowly.

To charge your iPad, simply connect it to a USB port – either on a computer or a USB power adapter. Note, however, that if you're charging via a computer, the USB port in question will need to be "powered" (most are these days). Also note that an iPad usually won't charge from a Mac or PC in sleep or standby mode.

When the iPad is charging, the battery icon at the top-right of the screen will display a lightning bolt. When it's fully charged this will change to a plug. If your iPad's power is so low that the device can't function, you may well find that plugging it in to charge will not revive it straight away – it should come back to life after ten minutes or so.

If you're in a hurry, don't use or sync the iPad while charging – this will slow down the process. For more on your iPad battery's life, see p.260.

The iPad at a glance

This diagram shows the third-generation iPad, which looks the same as the iPad 2. The first iPad has a slightly different layout.

Micro-SIM tray Gives access to the Micro-SIM card. To remove it, press the tiny circle with the supplied tool – or use a paperclip.

Headphone socket Takes standard stereo minijack plugs.

Mic (look for a small hole) Works well enough from a few feet away when dictating or using FaceTime.

Front lens (for FaceTime)

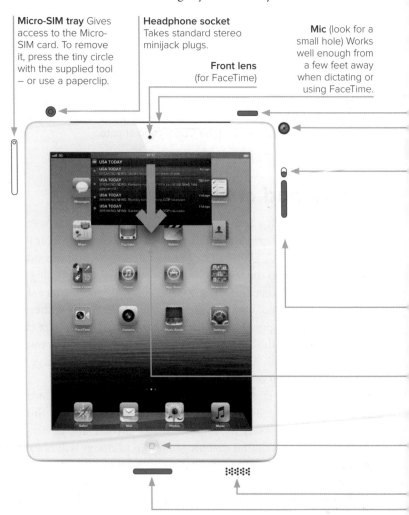

Sleep/Wake Click once to sleep; hold down for three seconds to power off.

Rear lens (for photos and video)

Lock Rotation/ Mute switch To select your preferred function for this side switch, look within Settings > General.

Status bar Displays the time and gives you feedback about your iPad via various icons. These include:

.ıll **Data connection signal level**. You'll also see the name of the current carrier you are connected to for data.

✈ **Airplane mode on**: data, Wi-Fi and Bluetooth signals disabled. To enable Wi-Fi in Airplane mode, go to **Settings > Wi-Fi**.

🔒 **Screen is locked.**

🔄 **Rotation is locked.**

▶ **Music or podcast currently playing.**

✦ **Location Services currently active.**

Data connections:

o GPRS (slowest)
E EDGE (slow)
3G 3G (fast)
LTE 4G LTE (faster)
4G 4G (fastest)

📶 ... which is replaced by this when connected to Wi-Fi.

✳ Bluetooth is on and paired. When grey, the paired device is out of range.

VPN A VPN network connection is active.

◎ Personal hotspot is active.

🔄 **Syncing with iTunes.**

🔋 **Battery charging.**

🔋 **Battery charged.**

Volume buttons Affect both music volume and also the ringer and alerts; look at the options within **Settings > General > Sounds**.

Notification area Swiping down from the top of the screen, as shown by the orange arrow, reveals a list of all your recent notifications, such as email and calendar alerts.

Home button Click to leave the app you are using and return to the last Home Screen you viewed. Whatever you're currently doing will be put on hold, so you can return to it later. Click again to go to the farthest left Home Screen. Click again to see the Search Screen (see p.74). Double click to see recently used apps (see p.73).

Dock connector socket Takes the iPad sync/ charge cable – which is interchangeable with a recent iPhone or iPod cable. The socket is also used for certain accessories.

Speaker Comes on whenever you play music, video or games with no headphones plugged in.

Staying in sync

Although the iPad works perfectly well on its own, there are lots of good reasons to sync it with other devices – such as your Mac or PC, or iPhone. This way, all your photos, contacts and other information will be available on all your devices at any time – and safely backed up, too. There are two main ways to sync the iPad with other devices, which you can mix and match as per your requirements. Neither is obligatory.

• **iCloud** Apple's online sync service, iCloud, provides seamless wireless syncing for the iPad, iPhone and iPod touch – as well as Macs and PCs. iCloud keeps your contacts, calendars, recent photos, documents from many applications and other data synchronized across all your devices. It also backs up your iPad and provides an online home for all the music, video and apps that you've bought from Apple, enabling you to easily install suitable apps on multiple devices. iCloud is free to use, though fees kick in if you need to sync and store more than a certain amount of data (excluding anything purchased from Apple, which is stored for free).

• **iTunes** Available for Mac and PC, iTunes is first and foremost an application for playing, arranging and downloading music, TV shows, movies, books, apps and podcasts. However, it has a secondary role as a control centre for your iPad. It allows you to sync music, video, photos and other data between your computer and tablet – and it also provides a fast way to rearrange apps on your Home Screens.

Syncing with iCloud

Launched with iOS 5 in autumn 2011, iCloud is an online service that supersedes previous Apple offerings such as MobileMe and .Mac. (The "cloud" of the title is a reference to cloud computing – a term used to describe technologies that make use of Web-based storage for data and applications.)

iCloud needs to be activated on each of the devices that you want to use it with. In each case you need to log in with an Apple ID.

> **TIP** In most cases it makes sense to use the same Apple ID for iCloud as you use for iTunes, though it's possible to have separate accounts – which can be useful if, for example, you share one Apple ID with your family for iTunes but each want to have separate contacts and calendars on your iPads and iPhones.

Where to find iCloud

• **On an iPad, iPhone or iPod touch** Log in when you first switch on or at any time later under **Settings** > **iCloud**. If you're using an older device, you might first need to upgrade to iOS 5 if you haven't already (see software update on p.258).

• **On a Mac** Open the **iCloud** section of **System Preferences**, which can be accessed via the Apple menu at the top-left of the screen. Note it will only work if you have a recent version of the Mac operating system – OS X 10.7 ("Lion") or later. If you have Lion but can't find iCloud in System Preferences, run **Software Update** (also in the Apple menu) to make sure you have the latest version.

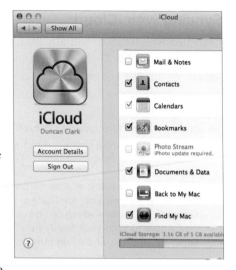

• **On a PC** If you haven't already done so, you'll need to download and install the iCloud Control Panel from apple.com/icloud/setup. Before downloading, check that your version of Windows is compatible and up to date.

• **On the web** You can access your iCloud account – and use various tools such as Find My iPhone (see below) – on the web at icloud.com.

Once logged in, your next task is to decide which parts of the iCloud service you want to use with each device. For many people, it makes sense to ignore the email option, which is only relevant if you're interested in setting up a new "@me.com" email address. But most of the other options are handy, including bookmarks, contacts, calendars, Photo Stream for recent pictures (see p.137) and Documents & Data, which allows iCloud-enabled apps to save files and other data directly to your iCloud account. On your iPad, you'll probably also want to enable Find My iPad, which allows you to find your device on a map using either the Find My iPhone app or icloud.com.

Once you've set up iCloud, everything should take care of itself: there's no need to manually tell it to sync.

Synchronizing with iTunes

If you've ever used an iPod or iPhone, you'll already be familiar with iTunes – Apple's application for managing music, videos and podcasts, ripping CDs, and downloading music and video. Although in most cases iCloud is the best way to sync contacts, calendars and bookmarks, you'll still need to use iTunes to upload music that you didn't buy from Apple, any video content, and photos from your archive.

If you already use iTunes

Even if you already use iTunes, you may need to update to the latest version to get it to work with the iPad. New versions come out regularly, and it's always worth having the latest. To make sure you have the most recent version, open iTunes and, on a Mac, choose **Check for Updates...** from the **iTunes** menu and, on a PC, look in the **Help** menu.

If you don't already use iTunes

All recent Macs have iTunes pre-installed. You'll find it in the Applications folder and on the Dock. Open it up and check for updates, as described above. If you have a PC, however, you'll need to download iTunes from Apple:

iTunes apple.com/itunes

   Once you've downloaded the installer file, double-click it and follow the prompts. Either during the installation or the first time you run iTunes, you'll be presented with some questions. Don't worry too much about these, but it's worth understanding what you're being asked...

• Yes, use iTunes for internet audio content or
• No, do not alter my internet settings
This is asking whether you'd like your computer to use iTunes (as opposed to whatever plug-ins you are currently using) as the program to handle sound and files such as MP3s when surfing the web. iTunes can do a pretty good job of dealing with online audio, so in general hitting yes is a good idea, but if you'd rather stick with your existing internet audio setup, hit No.

• Do you want to search for music files on your computer and copy them to the iTunes Library?
If you have music files scattered around your computer, and you'd like them automatically put in one place, select Yes and iTunes will find and import them all. Otherwise, hit No, as this option can cause random sound files from the depths of your computer to be imported – you can always remove them, of course, but it's usually nicer to start with a blank sheet and import only the files you actually want.

iPad
icon

Source List/
sidebar

Getting ready to sync – with and without wires

Once everything's up and running you'll be presented with the iTunes window. To the left is the Source List (sometimes called the sidebar), which contains icons for everything from playlists to connected iPads and iPhones. Click any item in the Source List to reveal its contents in the main section of the window.

By default, you'll only see your iPad in iTunes when it's physically connected, but you'll probably want to enable wireless syncing: this way you can sync whenever your iPad and iTunes are both connected to your home network. To do this, connect your iPad to your computer and under the iTunes **Summary** tab, check **Sync this iPad over Wi-Fi**.

Synchronizing

Whenever your iPad is showing up in iTunes, clicking its icon will reveal various tabs that control how the iPad is synchronized with the computer. These include the following, many of which are covered in more detail elsewhere in this book.

• **Info** Lets you synchronize contacts, calendars and bookmarks – though this is usually best left to iCloud. You can also sync mail accounts (i.e. login details and preferences), though it's normally just as easy to log into your mail on the iPad directly.

• **Apps** Lets you browse all the apps downloaded via your iPad or through iTunes. You can choose which ones to sync over to your iPad and even rearrange your apps into folders and across Home Screens – often quicker than doing it on the iPad itself.

• **Music, podcasts, video & TV shows** Lets you choose which of your iTunes content to sync over to your iPad. If you'd rather simply drag and drop music and video onto your iPad, rather than have it synchronized, click **Summary > Manually Manage Music and Videos**. Media downloaded directly onto the iPad, or playlists and track ratings created on the move, are copied to iTunes when you sync.

• **Photos** iTunes moves photos from your selected application or folder (see p.66) and gives you the option, each time you connect, of importing photos taken with the iPad's camera onto your computer.

• **Books** This is the tab where you choose how to synchronize PDF and eBook files (the latter in the ePub format) to be read on the iPad within the iBooks app. To find out more, turn to p.192.

Whenever your iPad is connected, you can click the triangle to the left of its icon in iTunes to see what music and other media it's currently storing. You can also click the triangle to the right of its icon to "eject it" and stop it displaying.

Forcing a sync from iTunes

When you choose from any of the above options, click **Apply Now** to start syncing straight away. You can also initiate a sync at any time by right-clicking the icon for your iPad (or Ctrl-clicking if you don't have a right-hand mouse button) and choosing **Sync** from the dropdown menu that appears.

Forcing a sync from the iPad

When set to sync over Wi-Fi, you can also initiate a sync to start from the iPad, assuming that it is on the same network as the computer running iTunes. To do this, go to **Settings > General > iTunes Wi-Fi Sync** and tap the **Sync Now** button. If syncing appears to be unavailable, go to your computer and initiate the sync from there, as described above – iTunes will then scan the network to regain the connection with your iPad so that the sync can happen.

Syncing with iTunes on multiple computers

When you connect your iPad to a different computer, it will appear in iTunes (as long as it's a recent version of iTunes) with all the sync options unchecked. You can then skip through the various tabs and choose to overwrite some or all of the current content.

• **Music, video, books & podcasts** Adding music, video, books or podcasts from a second computer will erase all of the existing media from the iPad, since an iPad can be linked with only one iTunes Library at a time. This applies even if you have **Manually Manage Music and Videos** turned on. You'll also lose any on-the-go playlists and track ratings entered since your last sync. Next time you connect at home, you can reload your own media, but you won't be able to copy the new material back onto your computer.

• **Apps** You can add and use apps from a second Mac or PC (even if it uses a different Apple ID) without overwriting existing apps on the iPad. However, you will need the Apple ID and password with which the apps were purchased.

• **Photos** These can be synced from a new machine without affecting music, video or any other content. However, to leave everything other than photos intact, you need to hit **Cancel** when iTunes offers to sync the "Account Information" from the new machine.

• **Info** When you add contacts, calendars, email accounts or bookmarks from a second computer, you have two choices – either merging the new and existing data, or simply overwriting the existing data. iTunes will ask you which way you want to play it when you check the box for a category and click **Apply**. However, you can bypass this by scrolling down to the bottom of the Info panel and checking the relevant overwrite boxes.

> **TIP** You can use multiple Apple ID accounts to make purchases on an iPad, but those purchases will only play back in iTunes on your computer if it is "authorized" for the account used (see p.170).

04

Getting to know your iPad

Settings and basic functions

Once your iPad is stocked up with all your media and data, you're ready to acquaint yourself with some of the basic settings controls, add a few personal customizations and generally make it your own. This chapter will also introduce you to a few really nice features of iOS 5, such as the Multitasking Bar and Notification Center.

Personalizing your iPad

Wallpaper

Tap **Settings > Brightness & Wallpaper** to choose the photo that appears on either your Lock Screen, your Home Screen, or both. Apple have a few ideas preloaded, but you can also choose from your own photos and drag and crop the image before setting it. When choosing a picture for your Home Screen, try to keep things minimal, as it can get pretty hard to deal with all your app icons over a busy image.

> **TIP** If you want a solid colour background, you'll need to roll your own using a painting app such as Brushes.

iPad name

You will probably also want to change the unimaginative name that iTunes gives your iPad during activation. To do this, tap **Settings > General > Name** and edit it. If you are syncing your iPad with iTunes, you can alternatively click on the name next to the iPad icon in the iTunes sidebar and retype whatever you want.

Sounds

Within **Settings > General > Sounds**, various sounds can be disabled. Keyboard clicks are the most likely contender … even if they don't bother you, they are probably annoying everyone around you. To use the iPad's side switch for muting the device, look within **Settings > General**. The alternate option is to use the side switch to lock rotation and mute your iPad from the Multitasking Bar controls (p.73).

> **TIP** You can also quickly mute the iPad's sound by pressing and holding the volume-down button on the device's edge.

Auto-Lock

Within **Settings** > **General** > **Auto-Lock**, set the number of minutes of inactivity before your iPad goes to sleep and locks its screen. In order to maximize battery life, leave it set to one minute unless you find this setting too annoying.

Passcode Lock

As already mentioned, if you want to protect the private data on your iPad – and make sure no one ever uses it without your consent – apply a passcode. Tap **Settings** > **General** > **Passcode Lock**, and choose either a four-digit number (a Simple Passcode) or something longer with letters and numbers. If you later forget the code, connect your iPad to your computer and restore it from the iPad **Summary** tab. If a thief tries this, they'll get the iPad working, but your private data will have been wiped.

> **TIP** Also found here is the option to automatically have all your data wiped after someone has tried, and failed, to unlock your iPad ten times. Though this is undoubtedly useful for some users, anyone with small children in the vicinity should probably avoid activating it.

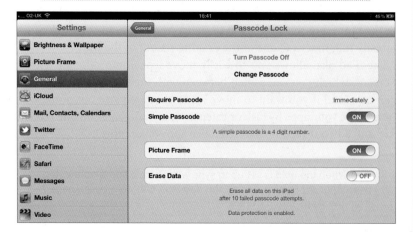

The Home Screens

The Home Screen is the launch pad for the iPad's various applications. The iPad can support multiple Home Screens; to move between the various screens, simply swipe a single finger left or right. Note that just above the Dock on each Home Screen is a row of dots that represents the number of Home Screens you have created, with the currently active screen highlighted.

> **TIP** You can also move between screens by tapping to either side of the Home Screen dots.

To rearrange the icons on the Home Screen, simply touch any icon for a few seconds until all the icons start to wobble. You can now press and hold any icon to detach it (you will see the icon lift slightly, as if stuck to your finger) and then drag it into a new position, or onto the Dock at the bottom of the screen. Up to six icons can live on the Dock; if it's already full, first drag one of the existing six out of the way.

The iPad also allows you to easily move icons onto different Home Screens, which you can switch between with the flick of a finger. This can be useful if you want to move icons you rarely use out of the way or arrange your apps by task or category (all your games on one screen, say, and all your reading and reference apps on another).

> **TIP** When the iPad is set up to sync with iTunes, and is connected (via either Wi-Fi or a cable), this process can also be managed from the **Apps** tab in iTunes.

Creating folders

You can also drag wobbling items onto other items to create folders, which offers a useful way of organizing things by category. When a new folder is created the iPad has a go at naming it for you; if you don't like what it comes up with, tap into the name field and type something else. To add further items to the new folder, simply drag them onto the folder's icon, and to remove items, drag them out.

Deleting apps from the iPad

To delete an item from the iPad, simply tap the ⊗ on the top-left corner of its icon. Annoyingly, you can't delete Apple's built-in apps, but you can move them to a screen or folder that you visit less frequently.

If you are deleting a whole raft of apps (maybe because you are running out of space), it is easier done from within **Settings > General > Usage**. Tap the apps in the list that you want rid of, and then hit the **Delete App** button. You can always sync them back again from iCloud or iTunes later if you decide you need them after all.

> **TIP** Once everything is laid out how you want it, click the **Home** button to fix all the app icons and newly created folders in place.

Adding websites

If you regularly visit a particular website – a newspaper or blog, for example – then add an icon (a "web-clip") for that site on your Home Screen. This way, you don't have to open Safari and tap in an address or search through your bookmarks each time you want to visit the site.

To create an icon for a website, simply visit the page in Safari and press ⬆. Select **Add to Home Screen** and choose a name for the icon (the shorter the better, as anything longer than around ten characters won't display completely on the Home Screen).

When you add a web-clip some websites will add a default icon to your Home Screen. If not, then the iPad creates an icon for it based on how the page was being displayed at the time.

> **TIP** To make the best-looking and most readable icons, try zooming in on the logo of the website in question before tapping the **Add to Home Screen** button.

The Home button

Whatever you are doing on the iPad, a single press of the Home button (the one physical button on the front of the iPad) takes you back into the Home Screens ... generally to the Home Screen that you last visited, if you have multiple screens running. A second press takes you to the far-left Home Screen; and a third press takes you to the Search Screen (see p.74).

When the iPad is locked, double-clicking the Home button displays the Music app controls at the top of the screen (including the option to use AirPlay (see p.185). However, when the iPad is in use, double-clicking the Home button (or using a special four-fingered Multitasking gestures, see p.74) does something far more interesting ... it reveals the Multitasking Bar at the bottom of the screen.

The Multitasking Bar

Multitasking is an important function to get to grips with when using the iPad, as it allows you to skip back and forth between apps without having to find them on the Home Screen. Additionally, it allows you to go back into an app in exactly the same place you were last time you used it, making it especially handy when copying and pasting between apps, referencing directions in an email on a map, etc. When opened, the Multitasking Bar displays the most recently used apps; if you need to find those used earlier, swipe to reveal more app icons located off-screen to the right. Tap one and you'll be taken to that app to pick up where you left off last time you used it.

If you need to remove an item from the bar (say you want to relaunch an app from its Home Screen icon), tap and hold any icon until they all start to wobble, then tap the red ● symbol. This does not remove the apps from the iPad, only from the Multitasking Bar.

Swiping in the other direction reveals a set of special controls off to the left (pictured): the Rotation lock/Mute button (see p.76), a brightness slider, Music app playback controls, a volume slider, and a shortcut to make the Music app appear full-screen.

Multitasking gestures

There are some very handy **multi-finger** gestures that can be used to really speed up multitasking on the iPad. These will work whilst using any apps, not just when looking at the Home Screen. While all of them work with either four or five fingers, they feel most natural when performed like this:

- **5-finger pinch** to return to the most recently visited Home Screen

- **4-finger swipe up and down** to show and hide the Multitasking Bar

- **4-finger swipe left and right** to move between recently used apps

If you don't get on with these gestures, they can be disabled within **Settings > General > Multitasking Gestures**.

Searching your iPad

When viewing the farthest-left Home Screen, the iPad's Search Screen is accessed by either a swipe to the left, or a press of the Home button.

Get into the habit of quickly popping to the Search Screen to find emails, apps, calendar events or contact details. You'll soon find that it can be much faster than navigating via specific Home Screens and apps. If you scroll right to the bottom of the search results for the content and data on your iPad, you'll also see two useful links to repeat the same search across the web, or more specifically, just Wikipedia.

To choose exactly what content from your iPad is searched, check and uncheck the options within **Settings > General > Spotlight Search**. Here, you can also change the order in which results are displayed, by dragging the ≡ icons up and down the list.

To back out of the Search screen, either tap the Home button again to get back to your farthest left Home Screen, or alternatively, swipe from right to left.

TIP If you tap the ⌨ key to hide the keyboard on the Search Screen, you will find the Dock lurking behind.

Wake/Sleep and On/Off

On the top edge of the iPad (when held in portrait mode) can be found the Sleep/Wake button. Just like its counterpart on iPhones and the iPod touch, this button can be pressed to put the iPad into Sleep mode (the screen will darken). A second press and the iPad wakes up to reveal the Lock Screen.

If you press and hold the button for a few seconds you are prompted to **Slide and power off**, which completely shuts down the iPad. Press and hold the button again until you see an Apple logo to turn back on.

> **TIP** Power the iPad on and off at least once a week and clear the Multitasking Bar to empty the iPad's memory caches and you'll find that it runs much more smoothly.

Picture Frame mode

Working much like a traditional screensaver, the iPad's Picture Frame mode displays a cycle of your photos on the iPad's screen. To kick things off, tap the flower icon to the right of the "slide to unlock" control on the Lock Screen.

Once running, tapping either the screen or Home button reveals the Lock Screen controls; tapping the flower icon again turns Picture Frame mode off.

Various options can be found for this feature within **Settings > Picture Frame**. The Origami setting is good fun; and you also get to choose whether you want to use all your photos or only a specific album.

Rotation Lock/mute switch

The iPad, like the iPhone and iPod touch, features a rotation sensor that turns the screen to keep its content upright as you rotate the device between portrait and landscape positions.

At any time you can lock the screen orientation (particularly useful when reading in bed) using either the physical side switch found next to the volume controls or the button that sits in the far-left position of the Multitasking Bar (see p.73). Both the side switch and Multitasking Bar button can also be used to mute the iPad, but you need to decide which way around you want the functionality to work. To set up your preference, look for the **Settings > General > Use Side Switch to** option.

Accessibility tools

The iPad comes loaded with several accessibility tools designed to aid the blind and visually impaired. To see what's available, and play with the options, tap through to **Settings > General > Accessibility**. Features include:

• **VoiceOver** Used to speak items of text on the screen. Touch an item to hear it spoken, double-tap to select it and use three fingers to scroll.

• **Screen zoom** Once set up, double-tapping with three fingers will zoom you in and out of the screen; dragging with three fingers moves you around the screen.

> **TIP** Interestingly, **Zoom** sometimes does a better job of rendering iPhone apps than the built-in 2x feature.

• **Color inversion** Renders the screen as a negative image, making blacks white, whites black, etc.

For those whose hearing is impaired, an option for turning on closed-captioning for video can be found within **Settings > Video**.

Also note the option for accessing various Accessibility controls via a triple-click of the Home button.

Notification Center

One of the best features to arrive with iOS 5 was the Notification Center, which is accessed by simply dragging down from the very top of the screen in either orientation. What you'll see depends on how you set it up, but typically the list of notifications would include all kinds of recent activity, from calendar alerts and unread emails through to app-specific items such as newsflashes or Twitter mentions.

To customize what you see in your Notification Center, tap **Settings > Notifications** and tweak the settings for each app in turn. In the same screens, you can also decide how you'd like pop-up alerts from each app to appear – with or without an icon, visible or not on the lock screen, and as a narrow banner or a larger alert with a dismiss button.

05

Typing & dictation

How to get the best from the keyboard and voice controls

The iPad's touchscreen keyboard isn't to everyone's taste, but once you get used to it it's possible to type surprisingly fast. Even more impressive is the good job that the iPad does of translating your speech into text when dictating. Following are some tips to get you started with both.

Typing basics

A good place to practise typing is in the built-in Notes app. Open it up and try the following techniques.

• **Using the keys** The iPad enters a letter or symbol when you release your finger, not when you touch the screen.

• **Numbers and punctuation** To reveal these keys, tap `?123`.

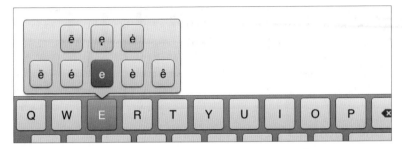

• **Symbols** To reveal these keys, tap ?123 followed by #+=.

• **Popover options** Many keys reveal useful alternative characters in little popover windows when you tap and hold. For example, tap and hold the letter "e" to reveal various versions of the letter with accents … simply slide to the one you want. Many symbol and punctuation keys also reveal alternatives when held, perhaps the most useful being the "!" key – when you tap and hold for a second or so, the key dishes up an apostrophe (slide your finger to it to select) without having to tap through to the numbers and punctuation screen.

• **Edits and navigating** You can tap anywhere in your text to jump to that point. For more accuracy, tap, hold and then slide around to see a magnifying glass containing a cursor.

> **TIP** In many instances you can banish the keyboard from view by tapping its ⌨ key.

• **Quick full stops** When you reach the end of a sentence, double-tap the space bar to add a full stop and a space. If this trick doesn't work, turn on the relevant option in **Settings > General > Keyboard**.

• **One-touch punctuation** Tap ?123 and then slide to the relevant key without taking your finger off the screen. Much more convenient than tapping twice.

• **One-touch caps** The same trick works with capital letters: tap **Shift** (⬆) and slide to a letter.

• **Caps Lock** If you like to TYPE IN CAPS, turn on the Caps Lock feature under **Settings > General > Keyboard**. You can then double-tap the **Shift** key (⬆) to toggle Caps Lock on and off.

• **Landscape keyboard** In Safari, Mail and many other applications, you can rotate the iPad to get a bigger version of the keyboard.

• **Thumbs and fingers** When using the iPad in landscape mode, use your fingers on the keyboard just as you would a regular keyboard. However, for portrait mode, experiment with holding the iPad with both hands so that you can type with two thumbs. It feels like a bit of a stretch at first, but actually works pretty well.

• **Split keyboard** If you would prefer an ergonomic split keyboard layout, look for the option within **Settings > General > Keyboard**. When enabled, tapping and holding the ⌨ key gives you the option to **Split** or **Merge**.

• **Undocked keyboard** With the **Split Keyboard** option enabled in **Settings**, the ⌨ key also offers the option to **Undock** the standard keyboard, which pushes it up to the centre of the screen. You may well find this a more comfortable position for extended periods of typing.

• **Keyboard shortcuts** One handy recent typing feature is the ability to create shortcuts for words or phrases that you use regularly. For example, you could specify an email address – such as johnsmith@gmail.com – and the iPad would then automatically offer up the address when you typed the first few letters. To add a word or phrase, tap **Settings** > **General** > **Keyboard** > **Add New Shortcut**. It's also possible to give each word or phrase a special shortcut, for which the iPad will automatically substitute the word or phrase each time you type it. For example, you could set it to replace "jsa" with "John Smith Associates".

> **TIP** To get your onscreen typing up to speed, check out a trainer app such as TapTyping.

Cut, copy & paste

In terms of typing, among the most useful features on the iPad are the **Cut**, **Copy** and **Paste** commands – especially if you don't particularly get on with the device's keyboard. Though at first they can seem a little fiddly to use, it really is worth getting acquainted with the taps and drags that bring these controls to life. And we are not only talking about text; these options will also pop up for copying images, and even entire webpages. For now, however, here's the deal with text:

• **Locate the text or word** you want to copy or cut and then tap and hold until an option bubble appears; choose **Select** to highlight that word, or **Select All** for the whole piece of prose. To speed things up, you could also try tapping once at the start of the text you want to select and then immediately dragging to the end of the last word.

Autocorrect and spell check

It's tricky to hit every key accurately on the iPad, but usually that doesn't matter much, thanks to the device's word-prediction software. Even if you hit only half the right letters, the iPad will usually work out what you meant by looking at the keys adjacent to the ones you tapped and comparing each permutation of letters to the words in its dictionary. However, no such system is perfect and the iPad does often get it wrong – sometimes with hilarious results, as sites such as damnyouautocorrect.com attest.

Accepting and rejecting suggestions

When the iPad suggests a word or name it will appear in a little bubble under the word you're typing. To accept the suggestion, just keep typing as normal – hit space, return or a punctuation mark. To reject it, finish typing the word and then tap the suggestion bubble before continuing.

Dictionary

The iPad has a very good built-in dictionary – including, for example, many names and swear words. In addition, it learns all names stored in your contacts and any word that you've typed twice and for which you've rejected the suggested correction. Unfortunately, it's not currently possible to edit the dictionary, but you can erase it and start again. Tap **Settings** > **General** > **Reset** > **Reset Keyboard Dictionary**.

To check the definition of a word you have typed, select it and choose **Define** from the bubble. If you need a second opinion, try an app such as Dictionary+ or the dictionary and Thesaurus app from Dictionary.com.

Spell check

After you've typed a word that the iPad doesn't recognize, it will be underlined in red to suggest that it might be a spelling error. If you want to check, tap the word and choose **Suggest** from the bubble, then select a word from the dictionary's presented alternatives.

Auto-capitalization

In addition to correcting letters, the iPad will add punctuation (changing "Im" to "I'm", for example) and capitalize the first letter of words at the start of sentences. If you prefer to stick with lower case, turn off Auto-capitalization within **Settings** > **General** > **Keyboard**.

• **Use the blue end-point markers** to resize the selection you have highlighted, and then when you are ready, tap **Copy** or **Cut** in the option bubble. Both actions move the selection onto the iPad's "clipboard", ready to be pasted elsewhere.

• **Navigate** to the place where you want to paste the text (which might be a completely different app, an email you are composing or perhaps the search field in Safari).

• **Tap and hold** at your desired point and choose **Paste** from the option bubble that appears. You can, alternatively, **Select** text (as above), then **Paste** over the top of it.

> **TIP** When copying, pasting and typing, you can undo your last action by shaking the iPad.

Other pop-up typing options

Besides cut, copy and paste, various other tools may pop up when you select text, depending on the app you're using. Tap the little triangle icons, where present, to see all the available tools. These include:

• **Formatting** Really useful when composing emails, you can add bold, italic and underline, as well as adjusting the quote level of each paragraph.

• **Suggest...** Presents similar words from the dictionary – useful if you ended up with the wrong word thanks to a dodgy autocorrect.

Dictation

Only available on the 2012 third-generation iPad, this tool is really easy to use and surprisingly effective. If you didn't choose to enable it when you first turned on your new iPad, look for the toggle switch within **Settings > General > Keyboard**.

Dictation does need the internet to work, however, as your speech recordings are processed on remote servers (hence the privacy notification when you first turn it on) and then the appropriate text is blasted back to your iPad in a matter of seconds. If you don't see the special dictation button to the left of the space bar on your keyboard, it probably means you are offline. Here are the basics:

• **Starting and stopping** When you want to dictate rather than type, simply tap the button and start talking very clearly at your normal level. When you are finished, tap again.

• **Punctuation** You can include punctuation verbally. Virtually any punctuation mark will work – from "comma" and "full stop" (which works better than "period") to "exclamation mark", "semi-colon", "dash", "asterisk" and even (for typography pedants) "en-dash" and "em-dash". You can also capitalize a word by adding "all cap" before it.

• **Make corrections** The results are generally pretty good, but you will need to dive in afterwards with the keyboard for a bit of editing and to add missing punctuation. Sections that the Dictation tool knows might be wrong get underlined in blue – tap these words to see alternatives.

Those with older iPads can download the excellent Dragon Dictation app, and then copy and paste text creations to whichever other app you need to use them in. And if you want a full-on speech-activated search assistant similar to Siri on the iPhone 4S, hunt down the charming Evi app in the App Store.

06

Connecting

Wi-Fi, Bluetooth and data networks

The iPad can handle various kinds of wireless signal: all models can deal with Wi-Fi, for internet access in homes, offices and public hotspots; and Bluetooth, for connecting to compatible headsets, keyboards and the like. Some iPad models also support 3G and 4G connectivity, for connecting when out and about, and out of reach of Wi-Fi networks. This chapter takes a quick look at each type of connection.

Using Wi-Fi

Connecting to networks

To connect to a Wi-Fi network, tap **Settings** > **Wi-Fi** and choose a network from the list. If it's a secure wireless network (indicated by the padlock 🔒 icon), the iPad will invite you to enter the relevant password.

It's best to have the iPad point you in the direction of Wi-Fi networks automatically. This way, whenever you open an internet-based tool such as Maps or Mail, and there are no known networks in range, the iPad will present you with a list of all the networks it can find. Turn this feature on and off via **Settings** > **Wi-Fi** > **Ask to Join Networks**.

If the network you want to connect to isn't in the list, you could be out of range, or it could be that it's a "hidden" network, in which case tap **Wi-Fi > Other** and enter its name, password and password type.

> **TIP** To view the signal strength of a connected Wi-Fi network, look to the 📶 icon on the iPad's Status Bar.

Forgetting networks

Once you've connected to a Wi-Fi network, your iPad will remember it as a trusted network and connect to it automatically whenever you're in range. This is useful but can be annoying – if, for example, it keeps connecting to a network you once chose accidentally, or one which lets you connect but doesn't provide web access. In these cases, click on the ⊙ icon next to the relevant network name within **Settings > Wi-Fi** and tap **Forget this Network**. This won't stop you connecting to it manually in the future.

When it won't connect...

If your iPad refuses to connect to a Wi-Fi network, try again, in case you mistyped the password or tapped the wrong network name. If you still have no luck, try the following:

• **Try WEP Hex** If there's a ⊙ icon in the password box, tap it, choose **WEP Hex** and try again.

• **Check the settings** Some networks, especially in offices, require you to manually enter information such as an IP address. Ask your network administrator for the details and plug them in by clicking ⊙ next to the relevant network name.

• **Add your MAC address** Some routers in homes and offices (but not in public hotspots) will only allow access to devices specified in the router's "access list". If this is the case, you'll need to enter the iPad's

Finding public hotspots

Many cafés, hotels, airports and other public places offer wireless internet access, though often you'll have to pay for the privilege of using them – particularly in establishments that are part of big chains. Typically, you connect and sign up onscreen. If you need to use these a lot, you may save time and money by signing up with a service such as BT Openzone, Boingo, or the services operated by T-Mobile and AT&T.

BT Openzone www.btopenzone.com
Boingo boingo.com
T-Mobile t-mobile.com/hotspot
AT&T att.com

The ideal, of course, is to stick to free hotspots. Try the Wi-Fi Finder app to help you locate them. Alternatively, browse an online directory such as:

Hotspot Locations hotspot-locations.com
WiFinder wifinder.com
Wi-Fi Free Spot wififreespot.com

MAC address – which you'll find within **Settings > General > About > Wi-Fi Address** – to your router's list. This usually means entering the router's setup screen and looking for something titled **MAC Filtering** or **Access List**.

• **Reboot the router** If you're at home, try rebooting your wireless router by turning it off or unplugging it for a few seconds. Turn off the Wi-Fi on the iPad (**Settings > Wi-Fi**) until the router has rebooted.

• **Tweak your router settings** If the above doesn't work, try temporarily turning off your router's wireless password to see whether that fixes the problem. If it does, try choosing a different type of password (WEP rather than WPA, for example). If that doesn't help, you could try updating the firmware (internal software) of the router, in case the current version isn't compatible with the iPad's hardware. Check the manufacturer's website to see if an update is available.

4G, 3G, GPRS and EDGE

In your home country, assuming you're in an area with network coverage, and assuming you have a data plan set up, a 4G- or 3G-capable iPad should automatically connect to your carrier's data network. When your iPad connects to the internet using the cellular data network, one of four icons will appear in the Status Bar: **4G** (which is fastest), **3G** (which is fast), **E** (for EDGE, which is pretty slow), or ° (for GPRS, which is slowest). Cellular data networks will automatically give way to Wi-Fi (which is usually faster) whenever possible.

Setting up data plans

Setting up a 4G or 3G data plan on the iPad is very easy, though the specifics of each carrier's plan may differ between territories. To get started, insert the Micro-SIM supplied by your network provider, then tap **Settings > Cellular Data**. Tap **Cellular Data Plan** and follow the onscreen instructions.

In many countries the iPad is unlocked, so you can go with whoever you like, assuming they can provide an appropriate data plan and a Micro-SIM card (smaller than a regular SIM card). In the US, however, you need to make a choice between AT&T and Verizon at the time you purchase your iPad. Check apple.com for providers offering suitable plans, and to check the situation in your country.

TIP If your iPad won't connect, ask your network provider to confirm the APN settings (**Settings** > **Cellular Data** > **APN Settings**).

Data usage and quotas

Depending on the territory in which you live, you may well sign up for a data plan that gives you a set amount of data usage each month (see p.45). The iPad will monitor your usage and warn you as you run out – at twenty percent, ten percent and zero remaining. When you go over your limit, either top up, or move onto a bigger allowance plan.

You can check to see how much of your data plan quota is left at any time by tapping **Settings** > **Cellular Data** > **View Account**.

TIP If you want to check how fast your connection is over either Wi-Fi or 4G/3G, download the Speedtest X HD app.

Connecting abroad

When overseas, you can activate international roaming within **Settings** > **Cellular Data**, but be aware that you may well get charged hefty roaming charges for the privilege if you use the same data plan you use at home. It's worth checking with your carrier to see what the situation is with partner carriers in the country you intend to travel to. A better alternative is to research the equivalent data plans in your destination country and pick up an iPad-compatible Micro-SIM card when you get there.

As for general internet access, Wi-Fi should work wherever you are – for free, if you can find a non-charging hotspot.

TIP 4G- and 3G-capable iPads feature a GPS chip that can locate your position even with data roaming turned off.

Airplane Mode

Only appearing on 4G- and 3G-capable iPads, the iPad's **Airplane Mode** is quickly accessible at the top of the **Settings** menu, and lets you temporarily disable cellular data, Wi-Fi and Bluetooth, enabling you to use non-wireless features, such as the Music app, during a flight, or in any other circumstances where cellular and wireless signal data use is not permitted. (Whether such signals actually cause any risk on aircraft is disputed, but that's another story.)

On many internal US routes these days Wi-Fi is made available within the cabin when the plane is at cruising altitude (i.e., the seat-belt signs are off). You will find that even with Airplane Mode enabled, you can go into **Settings > Wi-Fi** and turn it back on, allowing you to connect to the wireless network, but safe in the knowledge that all other connectivity remains disabled. You can do the same with Bluetooth (**Settings > General > Bluetooth**), if, for example, you want to use a keyboard during the flight, though do check with cabin staff before enabling it.

> **TIP** Owners of Wi-Fi-only iPads should make sure that Wi-Fi is turned off within **Settings > Wi-Fi** before take off and landing.

Bluetooth

Bluetooth allows computers, phones, printers and other devices to communicate at high speeds over short distances. The iPad's Bluetooth feature can be used to connect the device to certain peripherals, such as Bluetooth keyboards and headphones. A number of third-party apps also use Bluetooth to connect the iPad to the iPhone – the excellent Camera For iPad, for example, allows you to utilize the iPhone's camera, via a Bluetooth connection, to take photos remotely from the iPad.

You can turn Bluetooth on and off in **Settings > General > Bluetooth**. If you're not using it, leave it switched off to help maximize battery life.

Personal Hotspots – "tethering"

Although not everyone realizes it, it's possible to use a 4G or 3G iPad to provide wireless internet access to one or more other devices, such as laptops and other iPads. This can be enormously useful when you're out and about with a laptop and unable to connect online except via your iPad. Here's how it works: the iPad gets online in the normal way via the data network and then shares that internet connection with the laptops or iPads either via Wi-Fi (up to five devices), Bluetooth (up to three devices) or USB (one device). The only downside is that some mobile data network providers don't support "tethering" – as this function is traditionally known – and others charge extra for it.

If your carrier and tariff do support tethering, you can turn it on within **Settings** > **General** > **Network** > **Personal Hotspot**. Here you can also choose a password for the Wi-Fi network that will automatically be established by your iPad. Once that's all done, check your computer (or other connecting device) and you should see an available Wi-Fi network with your iPad's name. Select this, enter the password you chose and you should now be online. Alternatively, connect the computer and iPad with a USB cable or pair them using Bluetooth.

Connecting to office networks

Exchange – for calendars, contacts, etc

Most offices run their email, contacts and calendars via a system known as Microsoft Exchange Server. Individual workers access these tools using Outlook, and a web address is often made available to allow remote log in from home or elsewhere. If necessary, it's usually possible to access your work account via the web on the iPad – just press Safari and go to the regular remote-access web address. However, it's much neater to point your iPad at the Microsoft Exchange Servers directly – see p.104 to find out more.

VPN access

A VPN, or virtual private network, allows a private office network to be made available over the internet. If your office network uses a VPN to allow access to an intranet, file servers or whatever, you'll probably find that your iPad can connect to it. The tablet supports most VPN systems (specifically, those which use L2TP or PPTP protocols), so ask your administrator for details and enter them under **Settings** > **General** > **Network** > **VPN**.

Remote access

As well as connecting via a VPN, it's also possible for the iPad to connect directly to a computer that's on the internet – a Mac or PC in your home or office, say. Once set up, you could, for example, browse your files or stream music and video from your iTunes collection. All you need is the right app and the correct security settings set up on the computer in question.

There are dozens of apps available for this purpose; among the best are FileBrowser and PocketCloud Remote Desktop.

07

Apps

Downloading & organizing iPad applications

Perhaps the best thing about the iPad is the sheer number of applications – or apps – available for it. There are tens of thousands of apps out there, the vast majority of which can be downloaded inexpensively or for free. An app might be anything from a driving game to a metro map, from a tool for editing photos to a version of your favourite website optimized to work on the iPad's screen. If you can imagine an application for your iPad, someone has probably already created it and made it available.

Downloading apps

The iPad comes pre-installed with a bunch of apps – from Mail and Safari to Music and Videos. But these are only the tip of the iceberg. To see what else is available, dive into the App Store.

Just as the iTunes Music Store changed music-buying habits, Apple's App Store – which provides apps for the iPad, iPod touch and iPhone – is quickly changing the way in which software is distributed. With so many apps available, the main problem is the potential for spending more time and money than you meant to on them, and then having to figure out how to organize them all (see p.71). To use the App Store you'll need your Apple ID username and password (see p.165).

Accessing the App Store

• **On the iPad** Simply click the App Store icon. Assuming you're online, you can either browse by category, search for something you know (or hope) exists, or take a look at what's new, popular or featured. When you find something you want, hit its price tag (or the word "free") and follow the prompts to set it downloading.

Although apps can be downloaded via data networks, larger ones can take an eternity with anything less than a Wi-Fi connection.

• **On a Mac or PC** Open iTunes, click **iTunes Store** in the sidebar and then hit **App Store** at the top. All the same apps are available as when you access the store via the iPad. Any apps you download in iTunes will be copied across to your iPad next time you sync.

> **TIP** If you use iCloud, apps bought on any device, or in iTunes, can be made to appear on all your other devices automatically. To achieve this, log into iCloud on each device (**Settings > iCloud**) and then go to **Settings > Store** to turn on **Automatic Downloads**.

Different countries have their own iTunes Store, and you can only download apps from the Store in the region where your iTunes Account is registered. Note that there are no refunds in the App Store, so it pays to read reviews before you buy.

> **TIP** Be careful to choose apps that are suitable for the iPad – some apps are designed for the iPhone and iPod touch, and will run, but not look great (see p.19). Apps suitable for both are known as Universal Apps and marked with a **+** sign in the Store.

Buying apps with multiple accounts

Neither the iPad, nor iTunes on your computer, have to be wedded to a single Apple ID. So if more than one member of your household uses the same iPad, iPhone, Mac or PC, there's no reason why you can't all have your own IDs and buy apps separately. Once installed on the iPad, all the apps will be available to use, whichever account is currently logged into the iPad's Store. However, to update an app, you'll need the Apple ID and password for the account through which it was purchased.

> **TIP** To log out of your account on the iPad, either tap **Settings > Store > Account: name**, or scroll to the bottom of most App Store windows and tap your **Account: name** button.

Updating apps

One of the best features of the App Store is that as and when developers release updates for their software, you will automatically be informed of the update and given the option to install it for free, even if you had to shell out for the original download. To update apps:

• **On the iPad** The number of available updates is displayed within a red badge on the corner of the App Store's icon. Tap **App Store > Updates** and then either tap **Update All** or choose individual apps to update one at a time. To pause the download of any app update during the download process, tap its icon on the Home Screen.

• **On a Mac or PC** The number of available updates is displayed next to the Apps header in the sidebar of iTunes. Click **Apps** followed by **Check for updates**, bottom-right, to see what's available.

> **TIP** In **Settings > Store** you can decide if you want your Newsstand apps (see p.208) to update by downloading new content automatically.

• **In-app purchase** Many developers make additional features available through their apps as purchases, especially where the app may have initially been free to download. This can be a great way to extend an app's functionality. Purchases made in this way are charged to your iTunes account in the same way as when you buy an app from the App Store. To stop your kids from making in-app purchases, look for the option within **Settings > General > Restrictions**.

Checking app settings

Just like the apps that come pre-installed on the iPad, many third-party apps have various preferences and settings available. Many people overlook these options and can end up missing out on certain features as a result. Each app does its own thing, but expect to find some options and settings either:

• **In the app** If there is nothing obvious labelled Options or Settings, look for a cog icon, or perhaps something buried within a **More** menu.

• **In iPad Settings** Tap **Settings** on the Home Screen and scroll down to see if your app has a listing in the lower section of the screen. Tap it to see what options are available.

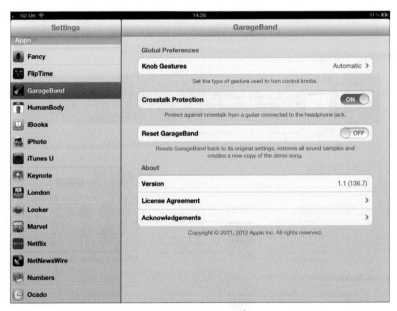

In this example Settings panel, for Apple's GarageBand, you get to both read the license agreement and acknowledgements and ... erm ... tweak your Knob Gestures.

Web apps and optimized sites

Whereas a "proper" iPad app is downloaded to your iPad and runs as a standalone piece of software, a "web app" is an application that takes the form of an interactive webpage, and so is accessed via Safari. The term is also often used to describe plain old webpages specially designed to fit on the iPad's screen without the need for zooming in and out. As such, you might also hear people refer to them simply as mobile-optimized webpages and websites.

Unlike many "proper" (aka "native") apps, web apps will usually work only when you're online. On the plus side, they tend to be free – and they usually take up no space in your iPad's memory. There are exceptions to these rules, however. For example, Google's Gmail web app uses a "database" or "super cookie" (see p.218) to store some information locally – which does take up space and enables some functions to be carried out even when the iPad is offline.

Several websites offer directories of optimized websites and web apps, arranged into categories, though increasingly many of these sites look out of date, due to the rise of fully fledged "native" apps.

iPad Web Apps ipad-webapps.com

Organizing apps

It's good to get into the habit of keeping all your app icons tidy using multiple Home Screens (see p.70) and folders (see p.71). But once you have lots of icons, you may find it easier to organize them in iTunes, which allows you to see multiple screens at once and to move icons around with a mouse. To do this, connect your iPad to your computer (either via a cable or Wi-Fi), select it in iTunes and click the **Apps** tab.

Deleting apps

Before you go deleting anything, it's worth noting that your Apple ID account keeps a permanent record of which apps you have downloaded, so if you delete both your iPad's copy and the iTunes copy by mistake, you can go back to the Store and download it at no extra charge by visiting the App Store on your iPad and tapping the **Purchases** tab.

If you delete a web-clip, you can reinstate it by restoring from a backup, though it is generally easier just to go back to the website in question and make a fresh one (see p.72).

You can't delete any of the built-in apps, but you can move them out of the way onto a separate Home Screen or into a separate folder if you don't use them.

• Deleting apps and web-clips from the iPad Home Screens
Hold down any Home Screen icon until they all start jiggling and then tap the small red ⊗ of the app you want to delete. When you've finished, hit the iPad's Home button. This will not remove the app from iTunes, so you can easily sync it back to your iPad again later.

• Deleting apps from the iPad's Settings panel Within **Settings** > **General** > **Usage** you will find a list of all the apps on your iPad arranged by size, making this the best way to delete apps if it's more storage space that you are after. Tap any app and then hit the **Delete App** button.

• Deleting apps from a Mac or PC Highlight **Apps** in the iTunes sidebar, then right-click the unwanted app and choose **Delete** from the menu that appears. If the app was also present on your iPad, next time you sync expect a prompt to either remove it from there too, or to copy it back into iTunes.

> **TIP** When asked to rate and review apps you are using, take the opportunity to do so; these ratings and reviews are displayed in the App Store for the benefit of other users.

Comms &
calendars

08

iPad email

How to set up and use email

Having email available wherever you are completely changes your relationship with it. Rather than being something you do when at your desk, the iPad makes email available to you on the couch, in the kitchen, In bed ... but unlike the experience of using email on a netbook or laptop, it is effortless and comfortable. And thanks to the additional screen real estate, the experience is a lot less fiddly than on an iPhone or other smartphone. As it is with Macs, the iPad's email application is known as Mail – and although the iPad version is much more limited than the Mac version, it has evolved into a great little app.

Setting up email accounts

The iPad comes pre-configured to work with all the most popular email systems – including iCloud, Yahoo!, Hotmail and, for corporate systems, Microsoft Exchange – without a time-consuming setup process. Gmail is also ready to go, but for the best possible service, set up your Gmail as an Exchange account using Google Sync (see p.106).

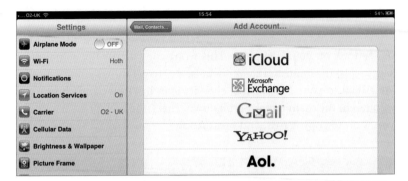

To set up an account the simple way, simply tap **Settings > Mail, Contacts, Calendars > Add Account**. Choose your account provider from the list and enter your normal login details. Under Description, give your email account a label, for example "Personal" or "Work" – this is your means of distinguishing between multiple email accounts within the iPad's Mail application.

You may be prompted to log into your account on the web and enable IMAP or POP3 access (opt for IMAP if given the choice). You can do this via Safari on your iPad, or using a computer.

> **TIP** Corporate email systems are usually based on Microsoft Exchange. This is fully compatible with the iPad – though it's up to your network administrator whether or not to allow access on iPads or other devices. Speak to them if you can't get it to work – and if they're not sure what the problem is, ask if they'd mind enabling IMAP on the server.

Setting up email accounts that aren't in the list

If you use an email account provided by an Internet Service Provider or some other system that's not already set up on the iPad, there are two ways to get that account up and running on your iPad – either copy across the account details from your computer using iTunes, or enter the details directly into the device.

Using iTunes

iTunes can sync your email account details between your iPad and Mail or Outlook on your computer. This won't copy across the actual messages – just the login and server details, etc. To get things going, connect your iPad to your Mac or PC, click its icon in iTunes and choose the **Info** tab in the main panel. Scroll down, check the box for each account you want to copy across, and press **Apply**.

Email jargon buster

Email can be collected and sent in various ways, the most common being POP, IMAP and Exchange. Here's the lowdown on each type:

• **POP** With a POP (or POP3) email account, messages can be sent and received via an email program, such as Mail on the iPad. Each time you check your mail, new messages are downloaded from your provider's mail server into your email program. It's a bit like a real-world postal service – and, indeed, POP stands for Post Office Protocol. When using a computer and mail program in this way, messages are usually deleted from the server as you download them. Though it is possible to leave copies "in the cloud", POP3 is really all about managing email with desktop applications.

• **IMAP** An IMAP account can also send and receive via an email program, but all the messages are based in the cloud, not on your computer. If you do use a mail program with IMAP set up, it downloads the email headers (from, to, subject, etc). Clicking on a message will download the full text of the message, but not delete it from the server.

• **Exchange** Exchange is Microsoft's corporate system. If you use Outlook at work, it's likely that you're using an Exchange email account; and, assuming your administrator allows it, you can set up an Exchange account so that you can access it via the web, from a home computer using a mail program, or from your mobile, smartphone or iPad.

• **Web access** Most POP, IMAP and Exchange email providers also let you send and receive email via a website. Everything resides in the cloud, and you read and compose your mail from within a web browser.

Entering the details on the iPad

To manually set up an email account on the iPad, tap **Settings > Mail, Contacts, Calendars > Add Account... > Other**. Then enter all the details for your account. If you're not sure of some of the entries – such as the mail server addresses – you can contact your email provider and ask them. If you'd rather not spend ages in a customer services phone queue, try searching the internet: most providers have a page on their website that spells out everything you need to know. It's also often possible to guess the details from the email address. If your email address is joebloggs@myisp.com, the username may very well be joebloggs (or your full email address); the incoming server may be mail.myisp.com or pop.myisp.com; and your outgoing server may be smtp.myisp.com.

Contacts and calendars too?

Some email accounts come with extra services such as calendars, contacts and notes. You can turn those on and off selectively for each account within **Settings > Mail, Contacts, Calendars**.

Some special kinds of contacts-only (such as CardDAV) and calendar-only (such as CalDAV) accounts can also be set up using the **Settings > Mail, Contacts, Calendars > Other** screen.

Push versus fetch

Traditionally, a computer or phone only receives new emails when its mail application contacts the relevant server and checks for new messages. On a computer, this happens automatically every few minutes – and whenever you click the **Check For New Mail** or **Send/Receive** button. This is referred to as a "fetch" setup.

By contrast, email accounts that support the "push" system feed messages to the iPad the moment they arrive on the server – which is usually just seconds after your correspondent clicks the Send button. iCloud and Yahoo! both support the push system for emails, contacts and calendars – and so do recent versions of Microsoft Exchange. If you use Gmail, you don't get push services by default at the time of writing – though it is possible to get them by setting up your Gmail account through Exchange using Google Sync:

Google Sync google.com/mobile/sync

You can turn push services on and off within **Settings > Mail, Contacts, Calendars > Fetch New Data**. Here you can also specify how frequently you would like accounts that use fetch to check for new emails. It's worth noting that the more frequently emails and other data are fetched, the quicker your battery will run down. These settings also apply to other apps (such as some to-do list tools and instant messaging clients) that rely on Apple's push services to grab your up-to-date data from a server.

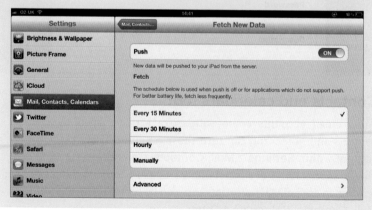

Using the Mail app

Using email on the iPad works just as you'd expect. Tap the Mail icon on the Home Screen to kick-start the application and then either hold the iPad in landscape mode to use Mail in a split-screen column view (with your inbox on the left) or in the portrait mode to see your messages full-width with a button at the top of the screen which reveals your inboxes or folders as a popover panel.

  With multiple accounts set up on the iPad, you get to view either your different inboxes individually or, very usefully, all together in a single list when you tap **All Inboxes**. Then…

• **Compose a message** Tap ☑ (If you have more than one account set up, first select the account you want to use from the list.) Alternatively, you can begin a message by tapping a name in Contacts and then tapping the contact's email address. At this point, third-gen iPad owners have the additional option of using the dictation function (see p.84) as an alternative to typing.

> **TIP** Although it's easy to miss, you can add formatting to your emails – including bold, italic and indented quotes. Tap to select some text and then tap ▶ on the popover to reveal the options.

• **View a message** Tap any email listed in your inbox to view the entire message. Double-tap, pinch and swipe to zoom in, zoom out and scroll, respectively. If you often find that you have to zoom in to read the text, try increasing the minimum text size under **Settings > Mail**.

> **TIP** Jump to the top of long emails or scrolling lists by tapping the iPad's Status Bar at the top of the screen.

• **Move between messages** Use the ▲ and ▼ buttons at the top to move up and down through your emails.

• **Move between accounts and folders** Use the left-pointing arrow button at the top (which displays the name of the item one layer up in the hierarchy) to navigate through all your folders and accounts.

• **Open an attachment** You can open (though not necessarily edit) Word, Excel, PowerPoint and iWork files attached to emails. You can also view images and PDFs from emails and save them to Photos and iBooks, respectively, from where you can sync them. To save an image, tap it and choose **Save Photo**. To save a PDF tap ↪ and then the **Open in "iBooks"** button, or **Open in...** if you have another preferred PDF reader app (see p.203).

• **Reply or forward** Open a message and tap ↩.

• **Move messages** To move one or more messages to a different folder, hit **Edit**, check the relevant messages and tap **Move**. Or, when viewing an individual message, tap the 📁 button.

• **Create a new Mailbox** In the Mail app "Mailbox" basically means either a folder or sub-folder in your hierarchy. To create a new one, go to the top level of your account, tap **Edit** and then, at the bottom, **New Mailbox**. Give it a name and choose a destination and then hit **Save**, and then **Done**.

• **Attach a photo** You can't add an attachment to a message that you have already started directly from Mail, but you can paste images that have already been copied using the **Copy** command in another application. To reveal the **Paste** command, tap and hold within the message you are composing. You can also create an email from images in the Photos app: select an image, tap ↰, and follow the prompts. To send multiple images from Photos while viewing a grid of images (either an Album, Places or Faces set), tap ↰ then select the images you want to

attach to an email and then hit the **Share** button. If you have multiple email accounts, messages that originate from Photos will be sent from the default account, which you can select from **Settings > Mail, Contacts, Calendars**.

• **Delete and archive messages** You can delete a message from a list by swiping left or right over it and then tapping **Delete**. To delete multiple messages simultaneously, tap **Edit** and check each of the messages you want to trash. Then click the **Delete** button. Note that iCloud and Gmail accounts may offer the option to "archive" rather than delete messages – though you can change this if you like (look within the **Advanced Settings** of a given account).

> **TIP** A third way to delete messages is to open them and press 🗑. This then jumps to the next message. If you don't want to waste time confirming each time you hit delete, turn off the **Settings > Mail > Ask Before Deleting** option.

• **Empty the Trash** Each email account offers a Trash folder alongside the Inbox, Drafts and Sent folders. When viewing the contents of the Trash, you can tap Edit and either permanently delete individual items or choose to **Delete All**. Alternatively, tap **Settings > Mail, Contacts, Calendars**, choose an account, and then tap **Account Info > Advanced > Remove** to set how often messages in the Trash are automatically deleted – either never, or after a day, a week or a month.

• **Create new contacts from an email** The iPad automatically recognizes phone numbers, as well as email and postal addresses when they appear in an email. Simply press and hold the relevant text to see the options to **Create a new contact**, **Add to an existing contact** or **Copy**. In the case of a postal address, you will also get the option to see the location in Maps.

> **TIP** As with Safari, you can tap and hold a link in an email to reveal the full destination address. Useful for checking the location of links before you click on them.

Tweaking the settings

Once your email account is up and running on your iPad, you can scan through the Settings to see what suits you. From the Home Screen, tap **Settings > Mail, Contacts, Calendars** and take a look at the available options. Here are a few things to consider:

• **Show** Use the **Show** option to determine how many messages are displayed within your Mail inboxes ... this is particularly useful if you are in denial about the amount of mail you have to get through.

• **Preview** Lets you set the number of lines of text that will be visible in your mailboxes for each message before you open it.

• **Show To/Cc Label** If you'd like to be able to see at a glance whether you were included in the To: or Cc: field of an email, toggle the **Show To/Cc Label** to the **On** position.

• **Organize by threads** With this option enabled, Mail groups all the email exchanges in a given conversation together, with the number on the right-hand side displaying how many messages are in the thread.

• **Always Bcc Myself** With some email accounts, messages sent from your iPad won't get transferred to the Sent folder on your Mac or PC. If this bothers you, because you want a complete archive of your mail on your computer, turn on **Always Bcc Myself** under **Settings > Mail, Contacts, Calendars**. The downside is that every message you send will pop up in your iPad inbox a few minutes later. The upside is that you'll get a copy of your sent messages next time you check your mail on your Mac and PC. You can copy these into your Sent folder manually, or set up a rule or filter to do it automatically.

• **Default Account** If you have more than one email account set up on the iPad, you can choose one to be the default account. This will be used whenever you create messages from other applications – such as when you email a picture from within Photos (see p.139).

• **Signature** Even if you have a sign-off signature (name, contact details, etc) set up at home, it won't show up automatically when you use the same account from the iPad. To set up a mail signature for your iPad, tap **Settings > Mail, Contacts, Calendars > Signature** and then enter your signature.

In some cases, you'll find extra options under the specific accounts listed at the top of **Settings > Mail, Contacts, Calendars**. For example:

• **Mail days to sync** Microsoft Exchange accounts offer this option for increasing or decreasing the number of days' worth of emails displayed on the iPad at any one time.

• **Archive messages** Available to Gmail and iCloud users, this option lets you choose which behaviour you'd prefer when you swipe over a message or tap the middle icon at the bottom of the screen while reading: either to delete the message (i.e. send it to the Trash) or archive it (i.e. send it to your Archive or All Mail folder). If set to delete rather than archive, you can still move messages to your Archive by tapping 🗂 and choosing your **Archive** or **All Mail** folder.

Email problems

You can receive but not send

If you're using an account from your Internet Service Provider (ISP), and you entered the details manually on the iPad, go back and check that you entered the outgoing (SMTP) mail server details correctly, and that your login details are right.

If that doesn't work, contact your ISP and ask for an outgoing server address that can be accessed from anywhere, or ask if they can recommend a "port" for mobile access. If they can, add this number, after a colon, onto the name of your outgoing mail server – which you'll find by tapping **Settings > Mail, Contacts, Calendars** and then choosing your account. If, for example, your server is smtp.myisp.com and the port number is 138, enter smtp.att.yahoo.com:138.

If you have more than one email account set up on your iPad, also try using an alternate outgoing mail server. To make sure that they are all available to be used by any given account, select that account, as above, and then tap **SMTP** and then toggle the other servers **On** within the **Other SMTP Servers** area of the panel.

> **TIP** If you're ever having problems with the Mail app, remember that in most cases you can also log in to your email directly via the web using Safari.

You can't send or receive mail from an account

Sometimes, problems can arise when multiple devices (an iPad, iPhone and Mac or PC, say) are all trying to access the same mail account simultaneously. This is sometimes referred to as a "lock-out" issue. Apple's advice is to close your Mac or PC's email application when not using it or, alternatively, set your iPad to fetch emails less frequently, via the **Settings > Mail, Contacts, Calendars > Fetch New Data** screen.

There are messages missing

The most likely answer is that your POP3 email account downloaded them to your Mac or PC before your iPad had a chance to do so. Most email programs are set up to delete messages from the server once they've successfully downloaded them. However, it's easy to change this.

First, open your mail program and view the account settings. In most programs, look in the **Tools** menu. Click the relevant account and look for "delete from server", which is usually buried under **Advanced**.

Choose to have your program delete the messages one week after downloading them. This way your iPad will have time to download each message before they get deleted.

Messages don't arrive unless I check for them

Unless you use an account that supports the "push" mail system, you are relying on your iPad's "fetch" settings to retrieve emails from the server. To check that it's configured the way you want, tap through to **Settings > Mail, Contacts, Calendars > Fetch New Data**. Of course, your iPad will also need to have an available internet connection (over either Wi-Fi or 3G/4G) to check in with your email account provider.

I get a copy of all the messages I send

It could be that **Always Bcc Myself** is switched on under **Settings > Mail, Contacts, Calendars**. This feature does have its uses, but it can also be very annoying.

Other email apps

Outlook Mail Pro

This elegant alternative email client is arguably the best in the App Store for integrating with an Outlook Web Access account. It has a really clean design, a decent enough feature set, and some tools for dealing with what it calls "problem servers".

Gmail

Google's free Gmail app is fast, easy on the eye, and has a very nice contrasting sidebar menu. If you use multiple Gmail accounts, you might also want to look at the feature-rich (but paid for) Safe Gmail.

Beware the phishermen

"Phishing" is a cunning form of online scam in which someone pretends to be from your bank, ISP or other such company, and asks you to hand over your personal information either directly or via a webpage. The classic example is a scammer sending out a mass email claiming to be from a bank, with a link pointing to a webpage purportedly on a real bank's website. In fact, all the details are slightly incorrect (for example, the page might be at www.hsbc-banking.com instead of www.hsbc.com). But the recipient might not notice and assume the email is legitimate, and so follow the instructions to "confirm" their online banking details on the fake site – in the process giving those details to a criminal who can then empty their account. The moral of the story is to never respond to emails – or instant messages – requesting private information, however legitimate the message might seem.

09

Other ways to connect

Calls, chats and tweets

Your iPad's front-facing camera allows video calls to be made over the internet using Apple's built-in FaceTime service. In this chapter we will show you how to get started with FaceTime, as well as its major competitor, Skype. There are plenty of other ways to connect using the iPad as well, including Apple's built-in iMessage app, so whether your thing is Twitter, Facebook or instant messaging, you're sure to find an app that suits your needs.

FaceTime

This service offers a free and relatively foolproof way of making and receiving video calls. FaceTime calls only work, however, when both people on the call have either an iPhone 4 or 4S, a second- or third-gen iPad, an iPod touch (with a front-facing camera) or the FaceTime desk-

top app (available from the Mac App Store; apple.com/mac/app-store) running on a Mac with a built-in webcam.

At the time of writing, due to the limitations of 3G networks in many countries, FaceTime will also only work when your iPad is connected to the internet via Wi-Fi, not 3G or 4G. Doubtless this will change in time, enabling iPad users to make video calls while they are out and about.

To enable FaceTime on the iPad, tap **Settings > FaceTime**, flick the **On** switch and enter your Apple ID and password; callers will then be able to reach you for FaceTime calls via your Apple ID email address. To contact your friends and family using FaceTime, you can use either an Apple ID or, with iPhone-using contacts, their phone number.

Once you have launched the FaceTime app, to initiate a video call, tap either **Favorites**, **Recents** or **Contacts** to browse for either Apple IDs or iPad 4 or 4S numbers that you want to call. You can also browse for FaceTime contacts direct from the Contacts app. Of course, your contacts will need to have FaceTime enabled on their devices (or running on their Mac) to receive your calls.

> **TIP** During the call, you can toggle between your iPad's two cameras using the ⟳ icon located at the bottom of the screen.

Skype

Skype, like FaceTime, is a VoIP (Voice over Internet Protocol) client; in other words, it makes calls via the internet as opposed to the traditional means used by the phone companies. With a Wi-Fi connection, you can use the Skype app, with a Skype account, to make free audio calls to other Skype users, anywhere in the world. You can also pay to call regular landlines and mobile phones. This can be very useful if your home phone is often in use, effectively providing a second line without any standing charge. Potentially, it can also slash your phone bills, especially if you regularly call long-distance. Skype also gives you a means of typing instant messages to other Skypers.

> **TIP** Skype also make the very handy Skype WiFi app, which lets you use your Skype credit to join thousands of paid Wi-Fi networks around the world.

iMessage

"Texting", also known as text messaging or SMS, is familiar to anyone who has ever used a mobile phone. However, on the iPad it works a little differently, as when you send a message (an "iMessage" no less) to another iPad, iPod touch or iPhone running iOS 5 (or a Mac user running the Messages Beta application), you do so over the internet, rather than a cellular data network. The main advantages of this setup are as follows:

• **Zero cost** iMessages are effectively free: you can send as many as you like without worrying about a monthly SMS allocation; they will hardly make a dent in any monthly data plan you have set up, and when used over Wi-Fi there will be no charge of any kind at all.

• **Receipts** When you send an iMessage, you'll get a delivery receipt to confirm that it reached its destination. And if the recipient has chosen to switch on read receipts (on the iPad in **Settings** > **Messages**), you'll also get a confirmation that they actually saw your message.

• **Not just phones** An SMS can usually only be sent and received by a mobile phone, but iMessages works with Macs, the iPad and iPod touch and also iPhones.

Using Messages

Clicking the green Messages icon reveals a list of unread messages (signified by a blue dot) and existing "conversations". Tap an entry to view one and you're ready to reply. Alternatively:

• **To delete a message or conversation** Swipe left or right over it to reveal the **Delete** button. Alternatively, tap ↪, highlight the messages you don't want and then tap **Delete**.

• **To write a new message** Tap ✎ and either enter an iPhone number, start typing the name of someone in your Contacts list to reveal matching names, or hit ⊕ to browse for a contact.

• **To send a message to multiple people** Start a new message (you can't do this via an existing conversation) and tap ⊕ to add new names.

Message notifications

When you have unread messages, the Message icon on the Home Screen will show a small red circle with a digit reflecting the number of new messages. You can also quickly access recently received unread messages by dragging down the notification area (see p.56).

Go to **Settings** > **Notifications** > **Messages** to adjust the options for how visual message notifications appear in both Notification Center and as alerts. For example, you may be at work and want to avoid message previews popping up (turn the **View in Lock Screen** and **Show Preview** option to **Off**).

Note that unlike a regular SMS message, recipients will be able to reply to all, as with an email.

• **To see if your message was delivered** Look for the **Delivered** label in small type underneath each message.

• **To forward a message** tap the ↱ button, then select one or more speech bubbles and choose **Forward**.

> **TIP** To quickly get to the top of a long iMessage conversation, tap the status bar at the top of the iPad's screen.

• **To quickly send a message to someone in your Contacts app** Scroll to the bottom of their entry page, tap the **Send Message** button, and choose their Apple ID or iPhone number from the list.

• **To add a photo or video** Tap the camera icon by the text area and either shoot a new pic or video, or choose one already on your iPad. (Alternatively, start by finding a video or photo you want to share, and tap the ↱ button followed by **Message**.)

• **To email someone from your Messages list** To see their other numbers and email address, click the 👤 button, top-right.

> **TIP** Street addresses, emails, web links or phone numbers in a text conversation can be tapped to launch Maps, Mail or Safari.

Contacts: your iPad's address book

Though perhaps not the most exciting thing to be found on the iPad, the Contacts app is arguably one of the most useful, especially if you find that you are using your iPad more and more like a digital Filofax. As well as names, numbers and addresses, the Contacts app has fields for all sorts of person-specific info, and because it keys in so well with the iPad's search feature (see p.74), it becomes an incredibly efficient means of retrieving contacts' details.

Using Contacts

Tap the Contacts icon on the Home Screen to get started. To browse the list, either flick up or down with your finger, or drag your finger over the alphabetic list on the left-hand edge to quickly navigate to a specific letter – useful if you have an extensive list of contacts. You can also return to the top of the list of contacts (or to the top of a long set of individual contact details) by tapping the iPad's Status Bar. To search for a contact, tap into the search field at the top and type in the first few characters of the name you're looking for. When you find the contact you want, tap once to view their details on the right-hand side of the screen. From there, you can…

• **Email a contact** Tap a contact's email address to instantly be presented with a blank email message addressed to that contact from your default account.

• **Go to a website** Tap a contact's web address listing to have the iPad switch to Safari and take you straight to that webpage.

• **View a map** Tap a contact's address and the iPad will show you the location in the Maps app (assuming you have an internet connection).

• **View Contact Groups** Tap the red **Groups** button at the top to view a specific set of contacts. Unfortunately, Groups cannot be created or edited on the iPad; they need to be set up on your computer before you sync.

• **Share a contact's details** Tap the **Share** button at the bottom to email someone a contact's details.

• **Copy any item** Tap and hold any field's entry and choose **Copy** from the options bubble that pops up.

By default the iPad sorts and displays your contacts by surname. To change this, tap **Settings** > **Mail, Contacts, Calendars** and then scroll down to the **Contacts** options.

Adding and editing contacts

Tap the ✚ button to create a new contact. To edit an existing contact – change their name or number, add an email address, or whatever – simply tap the relevant name in the main contacts list and hit **Edit**. Then...

• **Use the Add options** These are signified by a green ⊕ icon and are used to add a new number, address or other attribute.

• **Create new fields** If you can't see the relevant attribute, click **Add Field**. You'll then be offered everything from **Birthday** to a space for a **Nickname**.

• **Delete an item** To do this tap its red ⊖ icon. To delete the contact from your Contacts list entirely, scroll down to the bottom of the entry and tap the **Delete Contact** button.

• **Assign a picture to a contact** Tap **Add Photo** next to their name and then either browse the photo albums on your iPad for a suitable snap or take one with the iPad's camera. Once you've selected an image, you can pinch and drag to frame the snap just the way you want it. When you're done, click **Use**. To delete, edit or replace a photo associated with a contact, tap it and choose an option from the popover menu.

Apps for chat

Most of the main chat networks and chat clients have been busily pushing out apps since the launch of the iPad. Here are a couple to get you started:

BeejiveIM

BeeJive is a great chat app service, which allows you to chat simultaneously across a range of services (AIM, iChat, MobileMe, MSN, Yahoo!, MySpace, Google Talk, ICQ, Jabber and Facebook). It excels when it comes to notifications on your iPad, meaning that you always know when people are trying to contact you or have left a message.

IM+

This app is one of the best instant messenger clients currently available for the iPad. It supports live chat with friends on Skype, Facebook, Google Talk, Yahoo!, MSN, AIM, ICQ, and Jabber, and can also keep you connected to Twitter.

Textie Messaging

Similar in principle to Apple's built-in Messages app, this one also supports texting to phones over some cellular data networks in the US.

Emoji

If you want to use emoticons, also known as emoji icons, in your messages and emails, the easiest way is to download an app: Emoji is a good choice. Once it's installed, launch the app and then navigate to **Settings > General > Keyboard > International Keyboards > Add New Keyboard... > Emoji**. From then on, the new keyboard is available via the keyboard switching "globe" button to the left of the spacebar on your keyboard.

Apps for Facebook and Twitter

There are also many third-party apps with their own particular take on using Twitter, Facebook and the like. Here are a few worth checking out:

Facebook
This is the "official" way to use Facebook on the iPad. The app links well with the notification and alert features of the device, so you'll rarely miss anything that's going on.

TIP In the Facebook app's **Friends** tab there's a handy button for syncing your iPad's Contacts with your Facebook Friends list.

MyPad – For Facebook and Twitter
The iPad version of this app is particularly impressive. The ability to switch between Facebook and Twitter feeds in one place is really useful and works intuitively.

Twitter
Most Twitter clients do pretty much the same thing, so your choice is down to personal preference about how you want your tools laid out. This popular, and official, option is well designed, allows for multiple accounts and also boasts real-time search and a handy trending view.

Tweetbot
Dubbing itself a "Twitter client with a personality", Tweetbot is elegant and stable, with a full set of excellent tools and some intuitive swipe gestures.

TIP For even more apps, look within **App Store > Categories > Social Networking**.

10

Calendars

How to sync and use calendars on the iPad

More and more of us are switching from paper to digital diaries – not just for work, but for life, too. The iPad is helping to accelerate this trend by making it easy not just to schedule and manage appointments on the go – but also to view, edit and share multiple calendars and to synchronize them with laptops, iPhones and other devices.

Setting up and syncing calendars

Although it's possible to use the iPad as a standalone diary, most users will want to sync their iPad with their existing calendars on their Mac, PC, iPhone or with an online Google account. Here's how it's done.

• **iCal and iCloud** If you've already got calendars on your Mac in iCal – or on your iPhone – the simplest way to sync is to activate the iCloud calendar option on both your iPad and your Mac or iPhone.

• **Syncing via iTunes** If you use iCal but prefer not to use iCloud for some reason, it's still possible to sync them via iTunes (see p.104). Simply connect the iPad to the computer (either via Wi-Fi or USB), open iTunes, click the iPad's icon and switch on **Calendar Syncing** under the **Info** tab. This is also the approach to take if you have your calendars in Outlook on a PC. (For outlook on a Mac, see p.126.)

• **Google Sync** If you use Google Calendar, this can be easily set up on your iPad by setting up your Gmail account and switching on calendars (see p.103). The downside is that – at the time of writing at least – you'll only be able to see the mail calendar linked to your account, not any others that you've created, shared or subscribed to. If you want to get around this, one option is to use Google Sync, which bypasses the problem by serving up Google email, contacts and calendars via a Microsoft Exchange system. To get started, follow the (slightly fiddly) instructions at:

Google Sync google.com/sync

An alternative is to use a third-party app such as CalenGoo (see p.129) or to use the – actually rather good – web app version accessible with Safari at the usual Google calendar address.

TIP If you're struggling to set up a Gmail calendar that you only need to be able to view, rather than edit, consider subscribing to it instead – see p.126.

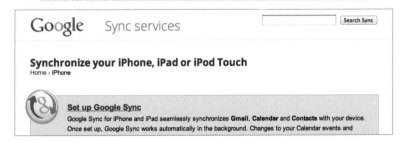

Google   Sync services   [   ] [Search Sync]

Synchronize your iPhone, iPad or iPod Touch
Home › iPhone

Set up Google Sync
Google Sync for iPhone and iPad seamlessly synchronizes **Gmail, Calendar** and **Contacts** with your device.
Once set up, Google Sync works automatically in the background. Changes to your Calendar events and

Syncing with Entourage and Outlook on a Mac

It isn't possible to directly sync calendars and contacts from either Entourage or the newer Outlook (which superseded Entourage with the launch of Office 2011 for the Mac). In order to enable syncing with the iPad, you first have to enable syncing between Entourage or Outlook and the Apple Address Book (called Contacts in Mountain Lion) and iCal (called Calendar in Mountain Lion).

To do this in Entourage choose **Preferences** from the **Entourage** menu. Under **Sync Services**, check the boxes for **Contacts** and **Events**. If you can't find these options, you may need to update your software. In Outlook 2011 it is basically the same scenario: look for the **Sync Services** options within the **Tools** tab to sync **Calendars** and **Contacts** to iCal and Address Book respectively, and then use iTunes (see p.125) to sync from there to the iPad.

• **Corporate account** Most corporate calendars are linked with a Microsoft Exchange account. To import and sync these calendars, simply set up the email account and switch on calendars (see p.105).

Once syncing with iCloud or iTunes is working, calendar data is merged between your computer and iPad, so deletions, additions or changes made in one place will immediately be reflected elsewhere (or the next time you connect to iTunes, if you're doing it that way).

Subscribing to calendars

The options described above are all about setting up calendar accounts in ways that enable you to add and edit events, as well as view events that already exist. However, it's also possible to "subscribe" to a calendar created by someone else. This is particularly handy for such things as sports fixtures and public holidays.

A quick Google search will reveal lots of options. When you've found one you want, grab the subscription address – which should be clearly shown on the website highlighting the calendar – and then add it to your iPad as a subscription. This is done by tapping **Settings > Email, Contacts, Calendar > Add Account > Other**.

Calendar on the iPad

The iPad Calendar app is very simple to use and doesn't require much explanation. You can view your schedule by year, month, week, day, or in a list.

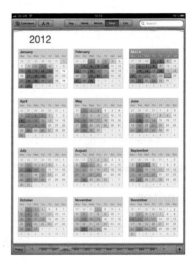

To add a new event, tap **+**, enter whatever data you like, and tap **Save**. To edit or delete an existing event, tap the relevant entry and use the **Edit** button. If you then want to delete an item, scroll to the bottom of the panel to find the **Delete Event** button.

Multiple calendars

You can have as many separate calendars on the iPad as you want. This is useful if you're syncing with a work and home account, for example, or if you want to have a specific calendar for a particular area of your life – childcare, for example, which might be shared between two parents. Each calendar has its own colour to make them easy to differentiate.

When you create a new event, you can choose which calendar it will be added to. If you don't specify, the event will be added to your default account, which you can set under **Settings > Mail, Contacts, Calendar**. To change an existing event from one calendar to another, tap it, followed by **Edit**, and use the **Calendar** option.

TIP As with emails, the frequency with which the Calendar app checks in with the server is determined by the "fetch" settings for a specific account. These settings can all be found within **Settings > Mail, Contacts, Calendars > Fetch New Data**.

Notifications

You can set an alert to remind you of an impending event either as it happens or a certain number of minutes, hours or days beforehand. To set up how these alerts appear – for example, in the middle or the top of the screen – tap **Settings > Notifications > Calendar**. To deal with the corresponding sounds that come with calendar alerts, look for the options within **Settings > General > Sounds**.

> **TIP** To quickly view upcoming events without opening the Calendar app, swipe down from the top of the iPad screen to reveal the Notification Center (see p.77).

Invites

Most types of calendar account support invitations. The person who created an event can invite other people to whom the event is relevant; if they accept, the event appears in their calendar too. To invite someone to an event,

tap the event, followed by **Edit > Invitees** and add some email addresses.

Incoming invitations can be accepted or declined via the invitations tray at the bottom-right of the Calendar app. The number of unanswered invitations shows up as a badge on the app's Home Screen icon.

> **TIP** You can decide whether or not incoming calendar invitations flash up on your screen under **Settings > Mail, Contacts, Calendar > Invite Alerts**.

Time Zone Support

Tap **Settings > Mail, Contacts, Calendars** and scroll down to find more Calendar-specific settings, including **Time Zone Support**, which controls whether the iPad displays events within the Calendar app for the time zone that the iPad's clock is set to (**Settings > General > Date & Time**) or for a Calendar app specific setting. If you're heading overseas for business meetings, it is essential that you get your head around how this works.

Other calendar apps

There are hundreds of calendar apps in the store – from apps created by specific sports teams and TV shows to apps for keeping track of lunar, solar and even fertility cycles. So if you're interested in anything date-specific, search the app store to see what's on offer.

Agenda Calendar

This calendar app is minimal and beautifully designed, with a very nice year-long "goal" view. The app integrates well with Notifications Center and features some nice multi-digit gestures for ease of use.

CalenGoo

This popular and colourful app syncs all your Google account calendars and offers a wide range of views.

Calendars – Google Calendars

This fully featured alternative calendar for your iPad, specifically designed with Google in mind, offers drag and drop event editing and SMS alerts. You can also zoom in the month view, making it easy to target individual events and see the detail (which many similar apps do not allow).

iPeriod for iPad

Allowing you to track dates, make notes and record symptoms, weight, mood, etc, this is your one-stop-shop when it comes to menstrual apps. And while many similar apps really go overboard with the pink and purple theme, this one is stylish and easy to use. The Pro version features graphing tools and is more customizable.

iStudiez

For organizing and viewing busy school or college timetables and calendars, try this excellent app (there's both a "Lite" and "Pro" version available in the App Store).

Calvetica Calendar

Feeding off the regular accounts that you might already have set up on your iPad or iPhone, this calendar app has a good set of tools under its belt and looks gorgeous.

Camera

11

Camera & photos

Shooting, organizing, viewing

The iPad is a great tool for carrying around your images and showing them off. Unlike a laptop, as soon as you start flicking through images, it stops feeling like a computing device and instead takes on the guise of an interactive picture frame. And though its built-in camera isn't going to replace a decent SLR any time soon, it does mean that the iPad is useful for quickly snapping stills and video clips.

The iPad camera

The third-gen iPad has two built-in digital cameras. There's a 5-megapixel stills camera on the back (the same as the iPhone 4 spec, while the 4S has 8 megapixels), which can also shoot HD video (1080p) at up to thirty frames per second. The camera on the front is not so hot, and is best reserved for video calls (see p.115).

Shooting stills

Launch the Camera app by tapping its icon on the Home Screen. To take a shot, aim and hold down the "shutter" button ⊙; release your finger at the moment you want to take the shot. As an alternative to using the onscreen "shutter" button, you can also use the physical "volume-up" button on your iPad to take pictures – figure out which method feels more comfortable for you. Now, try the following:

• **Hold it steady** The iPad takes much better pictures and focuses better when it's held steady, and when the subject of the picture is not moving. Try leaning on a wall, or putting both elbows on a table with the iPad in both hands, to limit wobble.

• **Keep the lens clean** Given that your iPad spends a lot of time with your fingers on its backside, the camera lense can get pretty smeary. If you find that many of the snaps you have taken look a little cloudy, invest in a microfibre cloth and give the lens a quick wipe before you point and shoot.

• **Set the exposure** To choose exactly which object or person you want the camera to base its exposure level on, tap on the screen to position the square focus target. Note that the iPad (third generation) can cleverly use facial recognition to determine when there are multiple faces in the shot and can then balance the exposure across up to ten faces at any one time.

• **Auto Exposure lock** If you tap and hold, the square target starts to flash to indicate that the exposure for your next snap is locked. Tap anywhere else on the screen to unlock the exposure and use the camera as normal.

• **Shoot outside** The iPad takes much better images outside, in daylight, than it does inside or at night. However, too much direct light and the contrast levels hit the extremes, resulting in a loss of detail.

> **TIP** Don't forget that you can rotate the iPad to shoot both still shots and video in either portrait or landscape mode.

• **Light source** Make sure that the light source is behind the camera and not behind the subject of the photograph.

• **Align with the grid** Tapping **Options** at the bottom of the screen reveals the **Grid** controls – useful for composing and aligning your subjects.

> **TIP** After taking a shot, swipe to the right to quickly preview the photo.

• **Get close and zoom** To take a decent portrait, you'll need to be within a couple of feet of the subject's face. This way more pixels are devoted to face rather than background; in addition, the exposure settings are more likely to be correct. Reverse-pinch the screen to zoom your frame, and to reveal the zoom slider.

• **Self-portraits** Tap the ⟲📷 button, bottom-right, to use the front-facing camera to take pictures of yourself.

> **TIP** One extra thing you can do with the camera is to shoot pictures of friends and family and then assign them to relevant entries in the Contacts lists, via the option behind the ↪ button. Annoyingly, though, you have to create a contact entry first (see p.120); you can't create a new contact directly from a picture.

Shooting video

To switch between stills and video shooting, toggle the little switch, bottom-right. Though you can't enable the zoom feature for video, from here on the process is pretty much the same as for stills, but with the addition of a glowing red light on the stop/start button to let you know when you are shooting.

As with stills, you can also use the physical "volume-up" button to stop and start recording. And, as you might expect, you can tap the ⟨📷⟩ button, bottom-right, to use the front-facing camera to film yourself – great for recording video blog posts.

The Camera Roll

The images and videos you take are saved together in the so-called Camera Roll, which can be found, when using the camera, by tapping the preview of your last shot, bottom-left. Alternatively, look within the Photos app. Videos appear here with a ◼◀ icon in their lower edge. Tapping the screen reveals additional controls and a scrubber bar for moving back and forth through the footage.

Note the **Slideshow** button at the top, which is used to kick-start a slideshow of all the photos in the Camera Roll. To delete, share, move (**Add To...**), copy or print (see p.248) photos from here, tap the ↱ button and then make selections by tapping the previews on the grid.

Putting existing pics on an iPad

The iPad can be loaded up with images from your computer. iTunes moves them across, in the process creating copies that are optimized for the phone's screen, thereby minimizing the disk space they occupy. iTunes can move images from an individual folder anywhere on your computer, or from one of three supported photo-management tools:

• **iPhoto (Mac)** apple.com/iphoto

Part of the iLife package, which is free with all new Macs (and available separately for $14.99/£10.49 from the Mac App Store). Version 4.0.3 or later will sync photos and videos with an iPad, but the most current version (9.2.3) is better, enabling you to view pictures according to the **Faces** in them and the **Places** they were taken.

> **TIP** If you sync your iPad with iPhoto on a Mac, when you connect the iPad to your Mac, iPhoto may automatically launch and offer to import recent snaps taken with your iPad. The way around this is to open **iPhoto > Preferences** and, from the **General** tab, choose **Connecting camera opens: no application** from the dropdown list of options.

• **Aperture (Mac)** apple.com/aperture

Apple's professional photo suite can do the job, but is pricier ($79.99/£54.99 from the Mac App Store) and though it does support Photo Stream and iCloud syncing (see opposite), is only really recommended to the dedicated photographer.

• **Photoshop Elements (PC)** adobe.com/photoshopelements

This Adobe app is similar to iPhoto, but with far more editing tools and a $79.99/£54.99 price tag. You'll need version 3.0 or later, but go for the current edition (version 10) as it has loads of nice editing tools.

All these applications offer editing tools for colour balance and so on, and allow you to arrange your images into "albums", which will show up in a list on your iPad. If you prefer, though, you can keep your photos within a standard folder, such as the **My Pictures** folder in Windows, or the **Pictures** folder in OS X. Any sub-folders will be treated as albums.

To get started, connect your iPad (via either Wi-Fi or a cable) and look for the **Photos** tab in iTunes. Check the **Sync Photos** box, then choose your application or folder. If you sync with a specific folder, any sub-folders will show up on your iPad as albums within the Photos app. Note the dropdown menu option that lets you choose exactly how far back you sync – useful if you have a sizeable photo collection.

iCloud and Photo Stream

With Apple's iCloud service (see p.18) you can temporarily synchronize photos (but not videos) across various Apple devices and computers. It doesn't sync all the photos in your collection to your iPad (there probably wouldn't be room), only the most recent 1000 shots that have been snapped on your Apple devices. It operates via the iCloud servers, but only over Wi-Fi or a wired network, so don't expect it to work over your carrier's data network. As a bonus, the 1000 photos don't count against your allotted iCloud storage limit.

To get started, make sure iCloud Services are enabled on your iPad (**Settings > iCloud**), turn on **Photo Stream** in **Settings > Photos**, then look for the **Photo Stream** album within the Photos app. On your Mac or PC, turn Photo Stream on within **System Preferences > iCloud** or the **iCloud Control Panel** respectively.

iCloud-synced Photo Stream images are automatically deleted from your Apple devices after thirty days, so if you want to make sure specific snaps stay on your iPad longer, view them in the **Photo Stream** section of the Photos app and tap ⤴, select the images you want to keep, tap **Save** and then choose where you want to put them.

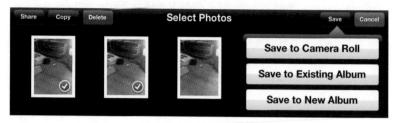

Photo Stream on a Mac or PC, however, does automatically import images into your image library prior to them being deleted from the Photo Stream album, making it an excellent way to make sure that all photos you take with your iPad do end up back on your computer.

Importing from an iPhone or digital camera

To do this you need an iPad Camera Connection Kit (which Apple sell for $29), which features two adapters. The first allows you to connect your iPhone or digital camera directly to the iPad's Dock connector using a USB cable (you are basically paying for a regular USB port), while the second is for inserting an SD memory card of the type found in many digital cameras. Once you have made the connection, the Photos application will launch so you can start importing.

> **TIP** If nothing happens, make sure your camera or phone is turned on, and if it has a special "import" mode, activate it.

Either tap **Import All** or tap to select the individual photos you want, and then tap **Import**. When the import process has finished you can choose to either keep or delete the photos on the SD card, camera or iPhone. To view the new photos, look in either **Albums > Last Import** or **Events > Today's date**.

The Photos app

Once your images are on the iPad, photo navigation is very straightforward. Start up the Photos app and choose from the various tabs – they are pretty self-explanatory, but tapping **Photos** shows you all the images in all albums, while tapping **Places** gives you photos with associated GPS location data represented as pins on a map.

TIP If you have synced photos from iPhoto or Aperture based on the Faces recognition tool, tap **Faces** to view the list. Unfortunately, the Photos app only displays synced Faces sets and cannot add to them as you take new photos.

Creating and deleting albums

From the **Albums** tab, tap **Edit** and then either:

• **Create an album** Tap **New Album**, give it a name and then select images from your iPad that you wish to include. You can always add more later using the **Add to...** command.

• **Delete an album** Tap the ⊗ icon on the corner of the album you want rid of. You can't delete either the Camera Roll album or any albums that you are automatically syncing via iTunes.

Options when viewing a set of images:

• **Share** Tap ⤴, highlight the images you want to send and then tap **Share** > **Email** to add them to an email.

• **Print** Tap ⤴, highlight the images you want to print, then tap **Share** > **Print** to send them to a local AirPrint printer (see p.248).

• **Copy** Tap ⤴, highlight the images you want and then tap **Copy**. The images can then be pasted into an email, text message or other document by tapping at the insertion point and choosing **Paste** from the pop-up panel.

• **Add to...** Tap ⤴, highlight the images you would like to be featured in a different album, then tap **Add to...** and copy them into either a new album or an existing one. This action will not remove the snaps from their original location.

When viewing individual images:

• **"Flick" left and right** to move to the previous or next photo.

• **Zoom in and out** Double-tap or "stretch" and "pinch" with two fingers.

Using the Photo Booth app

The other built-in app that hooks into the iPad's two cameras is Photo Booth. Again, there isn't that much to say other than launch it from the Home Screen and start playing. It basically takes photos (but not video) using various visual effects (such as **Squeeze**, **Twirl**, **Light Tunnel** and **X-Ray**) and then saves them to your **Camera Roll** album. As iPad tools go, it isn't going to make you look particularly sophisticated on a first date, but it does a fine job of keeping kids amused on long car journeys, and can be useful for creating amusing avatar portrait shots to be used on social networking sites.

- **Rotate the iPad** to see the picture in portrait or landscape mode.

- **Hide or reveal the controls** Tap once anywhere on the image.

- **More options** Tap ↪ to assign an image to a contact, send as an email, print, Tweet, or use it as wallpaper.

- **Start a slideshow** Tap **Slideshow** and then choose a Star Wars-esque transition and music if you want it. By default, the iPad will show each photo for three seconds, but you can change this by heading to **Settings > Photos**. The same screen lets you turn on **Shuffle** (random order) and **Repeat** (so that the slideshow plays around and around until you beg it to stop). You can also connect to a TV or projector via a cable (see p.184) or wirelessly to play your slideshows on a big screen. Look for available Apple TVs listed in the **Slideshow Options** panel.

- **AirPlay** Tap the ◺ icon at the top of the screen to view the current photo on a TV via an Apple TV device on the same network. You can then continue to swipe through the images on your iPad's screen and they will be mirrored on the television's screen. The ◺ icon will turn blue whilst the mirroring is active.

Native photo editing

When viewing an individual image in Photos tap the **Edit** button to see the available options. From left to right:

• **Rotate** Each tap on the **Rotate** button spins the image a further ninety degrees anticlockwise. Tap **Save** when you are done.

• **Auto-Enhance** Tap the **Enhance** button and this automatic setting does a pretty good job of tweaking sharpness, contrast, brightness and levels to get the most out of each shot. Tap **Save** when you are happy with the results.

• **Red-Eye** Tap the Red-Eye button, then tap each eye to remove that devilish glow. Tap the eyes again to undo.

• **Crop** Drag the corners of the onscreen grid to reframe manually, and use two fingers to twist if it needs a little realignment. Alternatively, tap the **Constrain** button for presets (recommended if you're going to want to print it at standard size). When you're ready, tap **Crop**.

Native video editing

You can snip the ends off video clips straight from a video preview in either Photos or the Camera Roll. Simply drag in the two end points on the scrubber bar (you'll see it turn yellow when you are in trim mode) and then tap the **Trim** button, top-right, when you're done.

Once you have finished editing your clip, note the option behind the 🔄 button to post your video straight to YouTube, where you can sign in using your regular Google login details (the same ones you use for other Google services, such as Gmail).

TIP For more sophisticated third-party photo- and video-editing tools available in the App Store, see the next chapter.

Online image posting from the iPad

Aside from Apple's own Photo Stream tool (see p.137), there are dozens of apps for photo sharing and uploading waiting to be discovered in the App Store. FlickStackr and Flickring HD are great choices if you use Flickr, the world's most popular photo-sharing site. Web Albums HD, meanwhile, is the stand-out app for Google's Picasa users.

It's also worth noting that the Facebook app (see p.123) and nearly all Twitter-interfacing apps (see p.123) also allow you to post images taken using your iPad's camera. If you've already entered the appropriate account details within **Settings > Twitter** on your iPad, you can post to your Twitter feed direct-ly from both the Camera Roll and albums within Photos. To do this, simply tap the 🔄 button when viewing a specific image and choose the **Tweet** option.

12

Apps: Photo & video

Making the most of your camera

There is a lot you can do with the iPad's cameras straight out of the box, but there's also plenty more to be discovered. Whether you want to craft near-professional quality photos, or re-create the look and feel of a bygone age of film-making, there are hundreds of apps out there to help you do it.

Camera apps

Mattebox

This app displays ISO, focal distance and the shutter speed of your iPad as you point and shoot. The image adjustments are not as sophisticated as on some other camera apps, but the shutter speed feature alone makes up for that.

FatBooth HD

This little app shows what you would look like if you were more interested in pies than iPads. After FatBooth becamean overnight sensation, its developers felt inspired to make iPhone apps (no "HD" iPad versions as yet) entitled AgingBooth, RobotBooth and BaldBooth … there are no prizes for figuring out what those apps will do to you.

Group Shot

Point your iPad at a group of people, take several shots and then use this tool to swap heads between the various images. It's a bit of a cheat, but a good way to rectify the pose of that one annoying person with their eyes closed who always seems to be there to plague such images.

Remotomatic Camera

This app gives you a Wi-Fi and Bluetooth remote control to be used with a separate iOS device on a tripod. It's great for remote and timed shots.

360 Panorama

This panorama app is easy to use and is backed up by a growing online community. Your panoramas are uploaded to the cloud where the images get automatically retweaked and processed, giving you an even better final product than you got on the iPad.

Long Exposure Photography

Use this piece of software to process snippets of video into single images, thus creating long-exposure shots. It works particularly well when you have the iPad mounted on a stand and when shooting pinpoints of light at night … say, photographing a motorway or kids with sparklers.

Image editing and adjustments

Though it's worth checking out the adjustment tools built into the Photos app (see p.139), there are plenty of other options out there for tidying up your shots.

iPhoto

With the arrival of the third-generation, Retina display iPad, Apple unleashed iPhoto as an iOS app. Its toolkit of filters and adjustments are very impressive, and the whole thing is managed using some very intuitive and clever gesture controls. For example, once you have specific colour adjustment or white balance tools enabled, simply dragging your finger up and down shows you the effect of the adjustment in real time. You can also post your images directly to Facebook, Twitter and Flickr from within the app.

Adobe Photoshop Touch

Anyone familiar with the professional desktop application is going to feel very at home here, with layers, adjustments, filters and standard selection tools all on offer. The touch gesture controls are really easy to use and the navigation intuitive. The app isn't free, but compared to the cost of the desktop version, it's an absolute bargain.

Snapseed

Another top-class app for adjusting photos and images to create some very professional results.

Tiltshift Generator

This app has an interesting toolkit of filters and blurs that re-create some of the hallmark effects of retro toy cameras, which used cheap lenses and were largely made from plastic. You can also use it for adding creative focus effects to your existing images. There is a very useful in-app tutorial and both Twitter and email sharing are supported.

Relievos

This app takes regular images and allows you to turn them into 3D "pop out" images. It works with some images better than others, and it's quite a tricky process to get the hang of, but once you've got a feel for it, the results can be very impressive.

Color Splash for iPad

Isolate and then colour and adjust individual sections of your images to create some novel results. The size and opacity options allow you to be very subtle with what you tweak and then, when you are finished, you can save your images back into your Camera Roll or post directly to Facebook or Twitter.

Video apps

iMovie
Great for adding sophisticated editing effects, transitions, themes, music and the like to your movies. Though some of the themes and the trailers feature are a little cheesy, the timeline and transition tools work well.

iSuper8
A really nice little app for shooting Super 8-style footage. Unlike the original format, you get the bonus of audio, and you can adjust various settings, including the frame rate and amount of "grain".

iStopMotion for iPad
All you need to make stop-motion animations at home. The app shows you the previous frame as you reposition your subject to create an impressively smooth effect. The same company also makes the free iStopMotion Remote Camera app, which lets you take the snaps using a Wi-Fi-connected iPhone (or another iPad) whilst previewing the animation on the iPad running the paid application. It's an awful lot of fun, and intuitive enough for both adults and kids to get to grips with.

Speed Machine
This video-shooting app lets you adjust the capture rate of your iPad so that you can create both slow motion and speeded up movie clips.

Music &
video

13

iTunes prep

Preparing music & video files to sync with the iPad

Downloading music and video from the iTunes Store (either direct to the iPad or to your computer) is all well and good, but if you already own the CD or DVD, there's no point in paying for the same content again. "Ripping" CDs and DVDs to get them into iTunes (and in turn onto the iPad) is easy, but it's worth reading through this chapter even if you've done it hundreds of times, as various preferences and features are easy to miss.

Importing CDs

To get started, insert any audio CD into your Mac or PC. In most cases, within a few seconds you'll find that the artist, track and album names – and maybe more info besides – automatically appear. If your song info fails to materialize (and all you get is "Track 1", "Track 2", etc), or you want to edit what has appeared, either click into individual fields and type, or select multiple tracks and choose **File > Get Info** to make your changes.

Settings and importing

Before importing all your music, have a look through the various importing options, which you'll find behind the **Import Settings** button on the **General** pane of **iTunes Preferences**. These are worth considering early on, as they relate to sound quality and compatibility. The iPad can play MP3 and AAC files (up to 320 kbps) as well as Apple Lossless, AIFF, Audible and WAV files (see box on p.152).

The bitrate is the amount of data that is used to digitally record each second of sound. The higher the bitrate, the higher the sound quality, but also the more space the file takes up. The relationship between file size and bitrate is basically proportional, but the same isn't true of sound quality, so a 128-kbps track takes half as much space as a 256-kbps version, but the sound will be only marginally different.

> **TIP** To rip multiple tracks as one, simply select them and click **Advanced > Join CD Tracks** before you import.

Take a quick look at the other options on offer, but don't worry too much as the defaults will do just fine. That said, the iPad only has a mono speaker (but does have a stereo headphone jack), so if capacity is an issue you could rip mono versions of your songs to use on it – they'll take up half the space of stereo versions.

When you are happy with everything in the **Import Settings** panel (pictured), hit the **Import** button in the bottom-right corner of iTunes.

Import Settings		
Import Using:	MP3 Encoder	⇕
Setting:	Higher Quality (192 kbps)	⇕

Details

96 kbps (mono)/192 kbps (stereo), normal stereo, optimized for MMX/SSE, using MP.

A Rough Guide to music file formats

Music can be saved in various different file formats, just like images (bitmap, jpeg, gif, etc) and text documents (doc, txt, rtf, etc) can be. When you import a CD to iTunes, you can pick from AAC, MP3, Apple Lossless, Wav and AIFF:

MP3 [Moving Pictures Experts Group-1/2 Audio Layer 3]
Pros: Compatible with all MP3 players and computer systems.
Cons: Not quite as good as AAC in terms of sound quality per megabyte.
File name ends: .mp3

AAC [Advanced Audio Coding]
Pros: Excellent sound quality for the disk space it takes up.
Cons: Not compatible with much non-Apple hardware or software.
File name ends: .m4a (or .m4p for protected files from the iTunes Store)

Apple Lossless Encoder
Pros: Full CD sound quality in half the disk space of an uncompressed track.
Cons: Files are very large and only play on iTunes, iPads, iPhones and iPods.
File name ends: .ale

AIFF/WAV [Audio Interchange File Format]
Pros: Full CD sound quality. Plays back on any system.
Cons: Huge files.
File name ends: .aiff/.wav

Converting one music file format to another

iTunes allows you to create copies of imported tracks in different file formats, which is great for reducing the size of bulky WAV, AIFF or Apple Lossless files, or for creating MP3 versions of songs that you want to give to friends who have non-Apple music players or phones.

To create a copy of a track in a different format, first specify your desired for-mat and bitrate in **iTunes Import Settings**, within the **General** pane of **iTunes Preferences**. Then, close **Preferences**, select the file or files in question in the main iTunes window and choose **Create MP3/WAV/AAC Version** from the **Advanced** menu.

When copying high bitrate songs to your iPad, you can set iTunes to convert them automatically to 128 kbps by checking the appropriate box under the **Info** tab of your iPad's options panel in iTunes.

Importing DVDs

As with music, before you can transfer video files to your iPad, you first have to get them into iTunes. In most cases, it's perfectly possible to do this from DVD, though in some countries this may not be strictly legal when it comes to copyrighted movies. As long as you're only importing your own DVDs for your own use, no one is likely to mind. The main problem is that it's a bit of a hassle. A DVD contains so much data that it can take more than an hour to "rip" each movie to your computer in a format that'll work with iTunes and an iPad. And if the disc contains copy protection, then it's even more of a headache.

> **TIP** Ripping Blu-ray discs is a prohibitively complex and time-consuming process. It's easier by far to hunt down discs that come with an accompanying digital version.

Using HandBrake

Of the various free tools available for getting DVDs into iTunes, probably the best is HandBrake, which is available for both Mac and PC. Here's how the process works:

• **Download and install HandBrake** from handbrake.fr

• **Insert the DVD** and, if it starts to play automatically, quit your DVD player program.

DVD copy protection

DVDs are often encrypted, or copy protected, to stop people making copies or ripping the discs to their computers. HandBrake does a pretty good job of dealing with such encryption, but if you find a DVD that trips it up, there are alternatives, such as AnyDVD (slysoft.com) for PC users and Fast DVD Copy (fastdvdcopy.com) for Mac users. These will leave you with a non-protected copy of the movie, which you can then rip for the iPad in HandBrake.

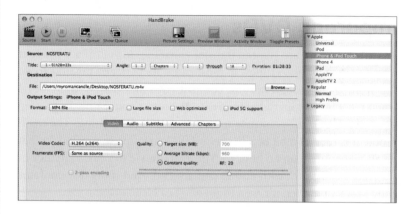

• **Launch HandBrake** and it should detect the DVD (it may call it something unfriendly like "/dev/rdisk1"). Press **Open**, and wait until the application has scanned the DVD.

• **Choose iPad-friendly settings** Choose the iPad option that relates to your model from the **Presets** menu.

• **Check the source** It's also worth taking a quick look at the **Title** dropdown menu within the **Source** section of HandBrake. Choose the one that represents the largest amount of time (say 01h22m46s) as this should be the main feature. If nothing of an appropriate length appears, then your DVD is copy protected.

• **Subtitles** If it's a foreign-language film, set **Dialogue** and **Subtitles** options from the dropdown menus behind the **Audio & Subtitles** tab.

• **Rip** Hit the **Start** button at the bottom of the window and the encoding will begin. Don't hold your breath.

> **TIP** Some DVDs and Blu-ray discs feature promotional codes that entitle you to a free iTunes digital version of the same movie.

Supported video formats

To get technical for a moment, note that the various video formats that the third-generation iPad supports include:

H.264-encoded video up to 720p at 30 frames per second, with AAC-LC audio up to 160 kbps, 48 kHz, in .m4v, .mp4 and .mov formats.

MPEG-4 up to 640x480 pixels, 2.5 Mbps, with AAC-LC audio up to 160 kbps, 48 kHz.

Motion JPEG (M-JPEG) Avi-wrapped and up to 1280x720 pixels, 35 Mbps, 30 frames per second with ulaw PCM stereo audio. (This is the video format often used by digital cameras that can also shoot video.)

• **Drop the file into iTunes** Unless you choose to save it somewhere else, the file will eventually appear on the Desktop. Drag it into the main iTunes window. This should create a copy of the new file in your iTunes Library, allowing you to delete the original from your Desktop.

Converting video files in iTunes

If you find yourself with video files in iTunes that can't be copied across to the iPad when you sync (perhaps they are the wrong file type you can easily convert them to an iPad-friendly format.

To do this for a video file, select it in iTunes and choose **Advanced > Create iPad or Apple TV Version**. After processing, the new file appears alongside the old one in iTunes and can then be synced over to the iPad in the normal way. Alternatively, download an iPad video playback app that can handle them (see p.189).

Store	Advanced	Window	Help
	Open Stream...		⌘U
	Subscribe to Podcast...		
	Create iPod or iPhone Version		
	Create iPad or Apple TV Version		
	Create MP3 Version		

Recording from vinyl or cassette

If you have the time and inclination, it's perfectly possible to import music from analogue sound sources such as vinyl or cassette into iTunes and onto your iPad. For vinyl, you could buy a USB turntable (such as those from Ion or Kam), but this isn't strictly necessary. With the right cables, you can connect your hi-fi, Walkman, MiniDisc player or any other source to your computer and do it manually.

• **Hooking up** First of all, you'll need to make the right connection. With any luck, your computer will have a line-in or mic port, probably in the form of a minijack socket (if it doesn't, you can add one with the right USB device; ask in any computer store). On the hi-fi, a headphone socket will suffice, but you'll get a much better "level" from a dedicated line-out.

• **Choose some software** Recording from an analogue source requires an audio editing application. You may already have something suitable on your computer, but there are also scores of excellent programs available to download. Our recommendations are GarageBand (the desktop version of the application, not the iPad app version), which anyone with an Apple computer purchased in the last few years will already have, and Audacity, which is available for both PC and Mac, easy to use, and totally free.

Audacity audacity.sourceforge.net

GarageBand apple.com/garageband

• **Recording** Connect your computer and hi-fi as described above, and switch your hi-fi's amplifier to "Phono", "Tape" or whichever channel you're recording from. Launch your audio recorder and open a new file. The details from this point onwards vary according to which program you're running and the analogue source you are recording from, but, roughly speaking, the procedure is the same.

You'll be asked to specify a few parameters for the recording. The defaults (usually 44.1 kHz, 16-bit stereo) should be fine. Play the loudest section of the record to get an idea of the level. A visual meter should display the sound coming in. If your level is too low, tweak your line-in volume level: on a Mac, look under **System Preferences** > **Sound**; on a PC, look in **Control Panel**.

When you're ready, press "Record" and start your vinyl, cassette or other source playing. When the song or album is finished, press "Stop". Use the "cut" tool to tidy up any extraneous noise or blank space from the beginning and end of the file; fade in and out to hide the "cuts", and, if you like, experiment with any hiss and filters on offer.

• **Drop it into iTunes** When you are happy with what you've got, save the file in WAV or AIFF format, import it into iTunes (choose **Import...** from the **File** menu), convert it to AAC or MP3 (see p.152) and delete the bulky original from both your iTunes folder and its original location on your computer.

Managing files in iTunes

Once you start digging around within the Music and Movies sync tabs in iTunes, it will soon become clear that the easiest way to manage your content for syncing to the iPad is by using playlists:

• **Regular playlists** To create a playlist, hit the **New Playlist** button (the **+**) at the bottom-left of the iTunes window. Then drag individual songs into the new list or add entire albums, artists or genres in one fell swoop. You can also create a new playlist by dragging selections into the sidebar, or by highlighting a bunch of material and choosing **File** > **New Playlist from Selection**. To add further tracks to an existing playlist, either drag and drop selections from the main iTunes window to the playlist's name on the sidebar, or, alternatively, right-click a selection and choose **Add to Playlist**.

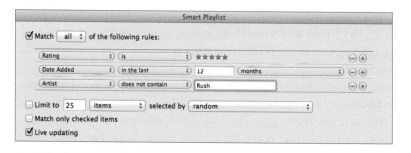

• **Smart Playlists** Rather than being compiled manually by you, these are put together automatically in accordance with a set of rules, or conditions, that you define. It might be songs with a certain word in their title, or a set of genres, or the tracks you've listened to the most – or a combination of any of these kinds of things. What's clever about Smart Playlists is that their contents will automatically change over time (assuming you tick the **Live updating** box), as relevant tracks are added to your Library or existing tracks meet the criteria by being, say, rated highly. To create a new Smart Playlist, look in the **File** menu or click the **New Playlist** button while holding down **Alt** (on a Mac) or **Shift** (on a PC) – you'll see the **+** button change into a cog.

Editing track info

A common niggle on the iPad and in iTunes is that you might end up with inconsistent labelling of track information. For example, you might find that you have one album by "Miles Davis" and another by "Davis, Miles". Thankfully, you can quickly edit this information. Simply select one or more tracks – or even whole albums, artists, composers or genres – and choose **Get Info** from the file menu.

TIP There are several applications that you can download to help with the clean-up process and find missing artwork. TuneUp (tuneupmedia.com) is a great choice for both Windows and Mac machines.

Home Sharing

Home Sharing is an iTunes feature that lets you stream the contents of your library across a home network to your other computers, iPads, iPhones and iPod touch. To get things started, open iTunes, then **Preferences** and, under **Sharing**, check the **Share my library on my local network** box. Next, click **Enable Home Sharing** in the iTunes **Advanced** menu. You'll then be prompted to enter your Apple ID – this will be the same one that you use in the iTunes and App Stores.

You are now ready to enable Home Sharing on your iPad (look within **Settings > Music**, and also in **Settings > Video**).

Syncing with the iPad

Once all your audio and video files are organized and ready to sync, connect your iPad to your computer using either a cable or wirelessly (see box) and check the boxes for the content you want to move across within the **Music**, **Movies** and **TV Shows** tabs of iTunes.

Take note of the options at the top of the **Music** tab. Don't check the **Automatically fill free space...** box, as this will limit your ability to download additional apps and music when out and about.

iTunes Wi-Fi Sync

Take the opportunity to enable Wi-Fi syncing (see p.63) while you are connected via a cable.Then, in future, you can sync without the physical connection. In iTunes, highlight your iPad in the sidebar and under the **General** tab check the **Sync with this iPad over Wi-Fi** box, hit **Apply** and then hit **Sync**.

Next, disconnect your iPad, make sure it is wirelessly connected to the same Wi-Fi network as the computer, and navigate to **Settings > General > iTunes Wi-Fi Sync**. Tap **Sync Now** to check that it is working. Syncing will now happen automatically when your iPad is connected to a power supply and on the same Wi-Fi network as the computer running iTunes.

If you try to load more music onto the iPad than there is space for, iTunes will ask if you want to create a playlist of the appropriate size and set it to sync. If you answer yes, iTunes will randomly fill a new playlist to which you can add and remove tracks in the usual way.

If you prefer, instead of having the iPad sync with a particular playlist or set of playlists (see p.157), you can move content to your iPad by simply dragging and dropping. To opt for this approach, click the **Summary** tab and check the box labelled **Manually Manage Music and Video**; then hit **Apply**.

Now you can drag tracks, artists, playlists or even whole genres (if you have the space) straight onto your iPad's icon from within iTunes. Clicking the ▶ icon to the left lets you see the contents of your iPad in more detail, allowing you to drag music into specific playlists.

With the iPad set up in this way, removing music is also handled manually, but don't worry: deleting a song from your iPad will not affect the original in your computer's iTunes library.

> **TIP** If you use iCloud then you might also want to set up iTunes Match (see p.167) as a means of mirroring your iTunes library to your iPad.

Moving music from your iPad to a computer

Automatic Downloads

If you want to have all the music purchases (along with app and book purchases) that you make from Apple on your iPad appear automatically back in your iTunes library then you first need to enable **Automatic Downloads** on your iPad (see p.167) and then, on your Mac or PC, open iTunes, make sure that your iTunes Store account password and ID are logged in (**Store > Sign in...**) and then open **iTunes > Preferences** and enable the options under the **Store** tab.

Manually transferring purchases

If you sync your iPad with iTunes via either a cable or wirelessly, right-click its icon in the iTunes sidebar and choose **Transfer Purchases from...** in the popover menu that appears. This will pull any purchases over from the device that are not already in your library.

If you connect your iPad via a USB cable to any other computer running iTunes the same right-click menu item is also available, allowing you to copy across music and video content downloaded from the iTunes Store. Of course, the content will only play back in iTunes if the computer in question is one of the five machines authorized for your iTunes Apple ID (see p.170).

Manually transferring other music

You can't copy music not purchased at the iTunes Store from iPad to computer. This setup is designed to stop people sharing copyrighted music, but can be a real pain if your computer is stolen or destroyed, and the only version of your music collection you have left is the one stored on your iPad.

Since the early days of the original iPods, many desktop applications have become available allowing iPad- iPhone- and iPod-to-computer copying. These have never been formally recognized by Apple, but they've generally worked well enough. Two worth investigating are The Little App Factory's iRip and Kennett Net's Music Rescue:

The Little App Factory thelittleappfactory.com
Kennett Net kennettnet.co.uk

14

The iTunes Store

Buying and renting, direct from the iPad

The iTunes Store isn't the only option for downloading music and video from the internet. But if you use the iPad, it's unquestionably the most convenient, offering instant, legal access to millions of music tracks and music videos, plus a growing selection of TV shows and movies to either buy or rent. Unlike some download  stores, the iTunes Store is not a website, so don't expect to reach it with Safari – the only way in is through either iTunes on a Mac or PC, or via the iTunes icon on your iPad's Home Screen.

What have they got?

At the time of writing, the iTunes Store boasts more than twenty million tracks worldwide, more than forty thousand music videos, plus over twenty thousand hours of audiobooks, many thousands of movies and TV shows, and over a million podcasts (see box on p.164). It claims to have the largest legal download catalogue in the world.

However, there are some glaring music and movie omissions, and it isn't like a regular shop where anything can be ordered if you're pre-pared to wait a while. As with any download site, everything that's up there is the result of a deal struck with the record label or movie company in question, and several independent record distributors have refused to sign up. So don't expect to find everything you want.

TIP To access the Store from a Mac or PC, click **Store** in the iTunes sidebar; once purchases have downloaded, you can then sync them to the iPad (see p.164) or use Automatic Downloads (see p.160) to have them appear automatically.

That said, thousands of new music tracks, audiobooks, TV shows and feature films appear week after week, so the situation is getting better all the time.

Podcasts

The best way to understand podcasts is to think of them as audio or video blogs. Like regular blogs, they are generally made up of a series of short episodes, or posts, which are nearly always free. Podcasts often consist of either radio-style spoken content or condensed documentary or chatshow-style video episodes, covering everything from current affairs and poetry to cookery and technology. There are many musical podcasts, too, though there's a grey area surrounding the distribution of copyrighted music in this way.

Podcasts are made available as files (audio or video) that can be downloaded either straight to your iPad or, alternatively, to a Mac or PC, from which you can sync them across.

Subscribing to podcasts from a Mac or PC

The iTunes Store offers by far the easiest method of subscribing to podcasts. Open iTunes, click **iTunes Store** in the sidebar and then click the **Podcast** tab to start browsing for interesting-looking podcasts. When you find one that looks like it's up your street, click **Subscribe**, and iTunes will automatically download the most recent episode to your iTunes Library. (Depending on the podcast, you may also be offered all the previous episodes to download.)

To change how iTunes handles podcasts, click **Podcasts** in the sidebar and then the **Settings** button at the bottom. For example, if disk space is at a premium, tell iTunes to keep only unplayed episodes. To sync your podcasts over to the iPad, connect it and look for the options under the **Podcasts** tab.

Subscribing to podcasts on the iPad

From the Home Screen, tap **iTunes** > **Podcasts** and browse just as you would any other department of the store. When you find something you want, tap the **FREE** button to start an episode downloading.

To play podcasts, by default tap **Music** > **More** > **Podcasts**. For the full story on podcast playback, turn to p.177.

If you want to stop your kids accessing podcasts through iTunes on your Mac or PC, check the relevant option under the **Parental tab** of **iTunes Preferences**. To do the same on the iPad, look within **Settings** > **General** > **Restrictions** > **Allowed Content**.

Shopping with your Apple ID

Though anyone can browse the iTunes Store on the iPad, listen to samples and watch previews and movie trailers, if you actually want to download anything you need to have a credit card associated with your Apple ID account and be logged in. If you haven't already done this: either try to buy something, and follow the prompts, or head to **Settings > Store** and enter the necessary details there.

If someone else is already signed in to the Store on the same iPad, they'll need to sign out first within **Settings > Store**. Also note that iTunes Store Accounts are country-specific; in other words, you only get to access the store of the country where the credit card associated with the account has a billing address.

TIP If you already have an Apple ID, iTunes Store, iCloud, iBookstore or AOL login, the same credentials will work here.

Staying secure

For Store purchases, the iPad will remember your Apple ID password details, by default, for fifteen minutes. If you have kids around, even this short period of time could be asking for trouble. If you want to set it up so that your password is required every time a purchase is made, enable **Settings > General > Restrictions** (make sure you remember the 4-digit pin you create for this) and then set the **Require Password** option to **Immediately**.

If setting up **Restrictions** seems like a chore, the alternative is to use a Lock Screen passcode (**Settings > General > Passcode Lock**) to control access to your iPad and the shopping opportunities therein.

TIP If you want to stop your kids accessing the entire Store on the iPad or being exposed to explicit material, look at the other options under **Settings > General > Restrictions**.

Renting movies

Many of the major movie studios are now making their films (both new releases and back catalogue titles) available to rent via the iTunes Store. Some films are also available in high definition (HD) with a slightly higher rental cost: these look amazing on the third-gen iPad's Retina display. Once a rented movie file has been downloaded to your iPad you have 30 days in which to start watching it, and once you have played even just a few seconds of it, you have a certain period of time to finish it (in the US it's 24 hours, in the UK, 48). When your time runs out, the file miraculously disappears.

A movie rented on the iPad can't be transferred to a computer or other device to be watched there. You can, however, rent a movie through iTunes on a Mac or PC and then sync it across to the iPad.

Annoyingly, you need to fully download an entire movie before you can start watching it, which, depending on your internet connection, could take a few hours. To see how your download is progressing, tap **More > Downloads** at the bottom of the iTunes Store window.

TIP To see trailers, read reviews and find local cinema show times, download the excellent free Movies by Flixster app.

Syncing purchases

Apple's various "cloud" services can give you access to your apps, iBooks and music (but not videos) via Apple's servers, on any of your Apple devices as well as your computer.

Setting up Automatic Downloads on the iPad

Assuming your iTunes account is logged in to the Store on your iPad, and you have enabled the feature within **Settings > Store**, then any music, app or book purchases you make on the device will be automatically synced to all your other devices and computer (assuming they also have **Automatic Downloads** enabled; see p.160 for how to do this within iTunes on a Mac or PC). This happens by default over

Wi-Fi, but can also be enabled over your iPad's carrier network via the **Use Cellular Data** switch (which might not be a great idea if you have a capped data tariff). It's a very useful feature, and because it works via your Store Apple ID, you do not have to have signed up to, or enabled, iCloud to benefit.

Setting up iTunes Match

But when it comes to music, that's not the end of the story. First launched in the US in late 2011 as part of the iCloud suite, the iTunes Match service extends your mobile cloud access to all the songs (up to 25,000) in your collection that you have *not* purchased from the iTunes Store (i.e., tracks ripped from CD or imported by some other means). Basically, iTunes determines which songs in your collection are already

Alternative cloud music services

Spotify

This paid subscription service, and accompanying iPad app (see p.179), give you access to an all-you-can-eat supply of music over the airwaves. However, you can also sync a selection of your favourite tracks to your iPad so that you can listen out and about without crippling your network data quota. The desktop application is excellent, and it lets you create playlists and organize your music in much the same way that you do with iTunes; you can even buy the songs outright if you want to. See: spotify.com

Amazon Cloud Drive

Amazon's cloud service gives you 5GB of free storage for all types of file, and any MP3s that you have purchased from their store are stored without eating into your allotted space. There is also the so-called Cloud Player that gives you access to your tracks from any computer connected to the internet. Though there isn't a Cloud Player app for the iPad, the web-based version works like a dream, giving you access to your tunes via Safari. Find out more on the website: amazon.com/clouddrive/learnmore

For other apps that give you access to music via your iPad, turn to p.176.

in the cloud (i.e. they are already on Apple's servers because they are sold in the iTunes Store) and automatically gives you access to them. Any tracks not "matched" are uploaded from your computer so that they are available for use in your iCloud library.

One of the pluses of this matching process is that your matched iCloud tracks (i.e., any track that was already in the cloud) will be at the high iTunes Plus quality (256 Kbps), even if the original tracks you have at home were ripped at a lower bitrate. On the downside, this service will cost you (see apple.com/itunes/itunes-match for the latest rates), and uploading unmatched tracks can take a while. It is also worth noting that while any kind of cloud service is great over Wi-Fi, it can be a real data-hog over a cellular network.

More in the Store

Here are a few other things that you might like to explore in the iTunes Store on either your computer or iPad:

• **Redeeming gift cards** If you are lucky enough to be given one, you can use iTunes Store gift cards and certificates to pay for content in the Store. To redeem a gift card, tap **Music**, scroll down, tap **Redeem** and follow the prompts. Your store credit then appears with your account info at the bottom of most iTunes Store screens.

• **Freebies** Keep an eye open for free tracks and video shorts: you get something for nothing, and you might discover something you never knew you liked. Also, make the most of the movie trailers on offer in the videos department; simply navigate to a file and tap **Preview**.

> **TIP** If you sync with iTunes, or use iCloud on both your iPad and computer, your purchases can be viewed in the **Purchased on...** playlist that appears in the iTunes sidebar.

• **Ping** This is Apple's music-based social networking service. It allows you to create a profile page and share your musical tastes with the world. You can also follow other fans, and artists, which can be a good way to discover new music.

• **iTunes U** iTunes U ("university") makes available lectures, debates and presentations from various colleges as audio and video files. The service is free and has made unlikely stars of some of the more entertaining professors. It was originally only a feature of the iTunes Store app, but has now also become a separate app in its own right, offering a wider set of educational tools, including access to custom courses, text books and device syncing.

DRM and authorized computers

All tracks in the iTunes Store come without traditional built-in DRM (Digital Rights Management) of the kind that Apple used to use to stop content being copied and passed on. Without the built-in DRM there are no technological barriers to someone distributing the files they have purchased. However, files downloaded from the iTunes Store do contain the purchaser's name and email details embedded as "metadata" within the file. The upshot of this is that files purchased from iTunes and then illegally distributed over the internet are traceable back to the person who originally shelled out for them. The other thing worth noting about iTunes-purchased files is that they're in the AAC for-mat, so they'll only play in iTunes, on iPods, iPhones, iPads and any non-Apple software and hardware that supports this type of file; unless, of course, you convert them to MP3 first (see p.152).

Apple also use what's known as FairPlay DRM, where content purchased using a specific iTunes Account can only be played on (or synced to, in the case of books and apps) a maximum of five Macs or PCs that are "authorized" for that account. (You can, however, add content to as many iPads, iPods and iPhones as you want; you just won't be able to move it onto a Mac or PC that has not been authorized.)

To manage the machines authorized for your iTunes Account, open iTunes on your Mac or PC and look for the options in the **Store** menu. To deauthorize the machine you are on (worth doing before you sell or get rid of a computer), choose **Deauthorize this Computer**. To deauthorize all machines and start afresh (useful if you no longer have access to one or more of your five), choose **Store > View My Account > Deauthorize All**.

• **Genius** Tap the **Genius** tab to get movie, TV show and music recommendations based upon items you've already bought.

> **TIP** The Downloads tab at the bottom-right of the iTune Store app's screen shows you the progress of any purchases currently downloading. Head here to restart uncompleted downloads if you fear that you might have lost your internet connection whilst downloading.

iPad audio

Using the Music app

The iPad doesn't feel like the most obvious personal music system in the world. You certainly aren't going to go out jogging with it tucked under your arm; and if you simply want a device for listening to music or podcasts on the move, a regular iPod or iPhone will serve your needs well enough. That said, the iPad's speaker is surprisingly powerful, and the Music app is pretty compelling.

The iPad's Music app

The iPad's built-in Music app (previously called the iPod app) is an easy-to-use, one-stop shop for playing music, podcasts, audiobooks and music videos. Tap the Music icon on the Home Screen to start.

From there on in, it really is self-explanatory: tap to see listings and then tap a track to hear it. You can also tap the artwork preview at the top to enter the full-screen artwork view.

Music app controls

Most of the controls are intuitive, need little elaboration, and can be accessed from both the main player view and the full-screen artwork view, but for those of you who have just landed from Mars, here's a run-through of what's on offer.

• **Pause/Play a song** Tap ❙❙ and ▶ respectively; or if you are using headphones with cord controls, click once.

• **To skip** to the start of the current or next song, tap ◀◀ or ▶▶. In a podcast or audiobook these buttons skip between chapters. You can also skip forward by quickly pressing headset cord controls twice; three quick clicks will take you back.

• **To see the track list** of all the songs of the current album when in full-screen artwork view, tap the ☰ button.

• **Scrubbing** To rewind or fast-forward within a song, slide the orange progress mark on the "scrubber" bar to the left or right. Alternatively, press and hold the ◄◄ and ►► controls.

• **To adjust the volume** drag the slider, top-right, to the left and right, or use the physical buttons on the side of the iPad.

• **Shuffle** Tap the ✖ icon to turn the shuffle selection feature on (black) or off (white).

• **Repeat** The Music app offers two repeat modes, which are available via the ⟳ icon. Tap once (it goes black) to play the current selection of songs round and round forever. Tapping it again (⟳) repeats just the current track.

• **Search** Type into the search field bottom-right and then tap between the **Songs**, **Artists** and **Albums** buttons to see results for each.

> **TIP** To quickly jump to the iTunes app from the Music app should you want to download additional music, tap the Store button, bottom-left.

• **Create a playlist** Tap **Playlists** > **New** and follow the prompts, using the ⊕ icons to add songs. To edit playlists, select one to view its contents, tap **Edit**, and then use the ⊖ icons to remove items, and the draggable ≡ icons to change the order of the list. There are also buttons to **Clear** the playlist's contents, or **Delete** it completely.

> **TIP** Playlists you create on the iPad will be moved across to your iTunes library next time you sync.

• **Stream music with AirPlay** Tap the ◱ icon to switch playback between your iPad's speakers and any remote speakers connected to an Apple TV, Airport Express unit or other device that supports AirPlay.

• **Star ratings** From the "Now Playing" screen, tap the ☰ icon and then slide your finger across the row of dots below the scrubber bar to add a rating for the currently playing selection.

> **TIP** Sync the music on your iPad from iTunes using a Smart Playlist of five-star ratings; you can then swiftly remove tracks you don't want by changing their rating on the iPad.

• **Genius** This feature generates a list of songs from your collection based upon accumulated iTunes Store information. In short, the Genius algorithms recognize that, for example, people who like The Beatles may well also like The Rolling Stones. Tap the ✻ icon to start.

• **Home button controls** Once music is playing, you can exit the Music app and continue to listen while using other apps. When the screen is locked, double-tapping the Home button reveals the Music play controls. When using other apps, double-tapping the Home button opens the Multitasking Bar (see p.73) where Music controls can be found by swiping to the right.

• **Shared Libraries** Tap the **More** button at the bottom to find additional sorting options and also the **Shared** button, which gives you access to other iTunes libraries on the same Wi-Fi network as your iPad. To let your iPad find your computer's library, go to iTunes on the Mac or PC and select **Advanced > Turn on Home Sharing.**

Deleting music from an iPad

You can't delete unwanted music directly from an iPad. Instead, simply delete the track in iTunes and it will be deleted from your iPad next time you connect and sync. Alternatively…

• **If you want the music on iTunes but not on your iPad**, uncheck the little box next to the names of the offending tracks, and in the iPad syncing options, choose "Only update checked songs".

• **If you don't want to uncheck the songs**, since this will also stop them playing in iTunes when in Shuffle mode, sync your iPad with a specific playlist and remove the offending songs from that playlist.

• **If you have Manual Music Management turned on** (see p.63) simply connect your iPad to iTunes via USB or Wi-Fi and browse its contents via the iTunes sidebar, deleting songs just as you would from a playlist by right-clicking and choosing the option from the dropdown menu.

> **TIP** In the case of videos, you can delete them directly from the iPad to free up space – simply swipe across and then tap **Delete** to confirm.

Music settings on the iPad

The iPad offers various options for audio playback. You'll find these by clicking **Settings > Music**.

• **Sound Check** This feature enables the iPad to play all tracks at a similar volume level so that none sound either too quiet or too loud. Because these automatic volume adjustments are pulled across from iTunes, the Sound Check feature also has to be enabled within iTunes on your computer. To do this, launch iTunes, open **Preferences** and under the **Playback** tab tick the **Sound Check** box.

• **EQ** Lets you assign an equalizer preset to suit your music and earphones. Note that you can also assign EQ settings to individual tracks in iTunes.

TIP For more sophisticated equalizer settings try playing your iPad music via the impressive EQu app, available in the App Store.

• **Volume Limiter** Lets you put a cap on the volume level of the iPad's audio playback (including audio from videos), to remove the risk that you might damage your ears or indeed your earphones. Tap **Volume Limit** and drag the slider to the left or right to adjust the maximum volume level. If you're a parent, you might also want to tap **Lock Volume Limit** and assign a combination code to prevent your kids from upping the volume level without your permission.

• **Group By Album Artist** A very useful setting for stopping complex "artist" listings set for specific tracks (say, where a song might "feature" someone else) fracturing the browsing experience of the "Artists" list in the Music app. Of course, for this to work, you need to make sure that you are making use of the "Album Artist" field in iTunes when prepping your library.

• **Home Sharing** Add your Apple ID here to be able to access shared iTunes music libraries (on a Mac or PC) on the same Wi-Fi network which are also enabled for Home Sharing using the same Apple ID.

The spoken word

For listening to your audiobooks and podcasts, the Music app is the place to go on the iPad. Playback works the same as with music, although you have a couple of different options available to you from the Now Playing screen:

• **Tell a friend (podcasts only)** Tap the ⤴ icon to send an email link to a friend so that they can find the podcast you are listening to in the iTunes Store.

• **Backtrack 30 seconds** Tapping the "30" icon, will rewind the audiobook or podcast by thirty seconds.

• **Playback speed** To adjust the playback speed of an audiobook or audio podcast, tap the "1x" icon to the right of the scrubber bar (to choose either "2x" or "½x").

16

Apps: Music

For fans, for musicians

For many people, the built-in Music app is as far as they want to take a relationship with music on their iPad. But there is plenty more out there, whether you want to play music, stream music or make music. It's worth exploring some of the other audio-related tools that litter the Music category of the App Store; in this chapter we pick out a few of the best.

Remote controls

The iPad is great as a remote control for any number of audio – and video – setups. Here are a few apps from the App Store that will help you get the job done:

Apple Remote

Free to download from the App Store, Apple's Remote app can be used to control iTunes on your computer via Wi-Fi. Coupled with an Apple Airport Express unit, this can be a great way to stream music using AirPlay from a computer in the bedroom, say, to your hi-fi system in the living room. It also works with an Apple TV unit connected to your television, allowing you to move around the onscreen menu system by swiping and tapping on the iPad's screen. For the full story on the Remote app, visit apple.com/itunes/remote, and for more information about Apple TV, point your browser at apple.com/appletv.

Rowmote Pro

Though it'll cost you a few dollars, this super-charged app is worth having a play with, as it gives you control of all sorts of applications on your Mac computer, not just iTunes.

TIP There are also loads of third-party remotes in the App Store for controlling Spotify playback; a good choice is Remoteless (for Spotify).

Apps for listening to music

Spotify

With a subscription, you can stream unlimited music to this app from the internet (and also play downloaded selections offline) for around the price of a CD album per month. Without the premium account, you can stream music to the app from your desktop (a bit like Home Sharing). Though not yet available in every country, it's pretty compelling for those who can get it.

TuneIn Radio

This is a great radio tuner app. It offers more than 40,000 stations, and loads of useful features, including a sleep timer, pause and rewind controls, and a filter tool that chooses stations for you based on your music library content.

VinylLove

For the nostalgic among you, this virtual turntable lets you listen to the music on your iPad with a little added crackle. You also get to move the turntable's arm to choose the track, or position within the track.

Virtual instruments

The Music category within the App Store is awash with virtual instruments, sequencers, drum pads and other noisy creations. With a bit of perseverance and a sprinkling of talent there are some that can be made to sound more than just a novelty. Here are a few worth looking at:

GuitarToolKit

When the App Store was first launched the world was wowed by virtual guitar apps. A few years on and there are hundreds available. This is one of the best, complete with a tuner and metronome to help you play one of those old-skool wooden versions.

Seline Ultimate

Both a unique ergonomic playing environment and an amazing selection of synthesized instruments, filters and audio tweaking tools. The app is also fully MIDI compatible, meaning you can hook it up to a real keyboard and play it using conventional keys. Though there is more than enough to keep you busy for a long time, the in-app purchase library includes extra loops, drones and tones.

Piano / Piano Tunes

Nice-sounding (and many aren't) piano app with tunes to learn. Piano is free, while Piano Tunes is paid and ad-free.

NLog MIDI Synth
Arguably the best Korg-styled tone generator for the iPhone and iPad, with a delightful analogue feel to the interface.

TIP Remember that the headphone jack can be used as a line-out to play your creations via a PA, amplifier or hi-fi system instead of the iPad's built-in speaker.

TNR-i
Innovative instrument that uses a grid of glowing buttons to create electronic music. When signed into Games Center you can also participate in online jam sessions.

Studio solutions

BeatMaker 2
Featuring a drum machine, sequencer, keyboard, mixer, wave editor, and more, this app is an undisputed bargain.

GarageBand
Apple's all-in-one music creation package comes into its own on the iPad. There are both virtual instruments and so-called "smart"-instruments (which pretty much play themselves for you) and a very swish multitrack mixing environment with a plethora of filters and adjustment.

NanoStudio
Before making a final decision on which iPad recording studio is going to suit you, check out this contender. The added ability to upload straight to SoundCloud is a useful bonus.

Miscellaneous

Songsterr Plus

More guitar and drum kit tabs laid out in one place than you could shake a stick at. It also features a built-in guitar engine, so that you can hear what the tab should sound like before you have a stab, and a control for adjusting the tab scroll speed.

Nota For iPad

A fantastic music theory app, featuring a piano chord and scale browser, a landscape keyboard for practising, and a quiz for testing your progress.

Discovr Music

An essential download for all music lovers, this app shows you all the bands that it thinks you might like based on your favourite artists and genre choices. You can watch the bands' videos and hear song previews – it's a great way to find new music.

SoundHound

There are many music recognition apps out there that can hear any song playing and tell you what it is. Shazam is arguably the best-known, but SoundHound is our recommendation. Aside from being fast and reliable, it even does a pretty good job of recognizing hummed tunes as well as the recorded originals. There's also a paid version without ads.

iPad video

Using the built-in apps

The iPad's screen is great for watching video: it's not so small that it's a strain to watch, but not so big that it can't be snuggled up with in bed to watch a movie.

Playing videos

To watch videos on the iPad, head to the Videos app and start browsing the categories. Depending on the content you have either downloaded from the iTunes Store or synced across from iTunes, you'll find categories such as **Movies**, **TV Shows**, **Podcasts** and **Music** **Videos**. Also note the **Shared** tab, which gives access to libraries of video made available via Home Sharing (see p.159). A grey dot next to an episode in a season list on the iPad means that the file has not yet been viewed. Tap an item to start playback. Once the video is playing, tapping the screen reveals play, volume and scrubbing controls, just like for audio. Additionally, you can:

• **Toggle views** Tap the ▬ and ▣ icons to toggle between theatrical widescreen and full-screen (cropped) views.

> **TIP** You can also toggle between the two view modes by simply double-tapping the screen.

• **Display subtitles** Where the file you are watching supports them, tap the 🗩 icon to the left of the play controls to access audio and subtitles options for the playing movie.

• **Display chapters** Where the file you are watching supports them, tap the ☰ icon to the right of the play controls to display the chapters of the movie you are watching.

• **Delete files** To delete a movie from the iPad (which can be really handy if you want to make space for more content when out and about), simply swipe across its entry and then tap **Delete** to confirm.

> **TIP** For additional video playback options and settings, look within **Settings > Video**.

Video out

The iPad can output both NTSC and PAL TV signals so that you can connect your iPad to a TV or projector. This can be done using one of the following, which all attach to the iPad via the Dock connector:

• **Apple iPad Dock Connector to VGA Adapter** This is great for connecting to most standard projectors.

• **Apple iPad Dock Connector to HDMI Adapter** This is useful for connecting to most modern TV and projector setups.

• **Apple Component AV Cable** This gives you five RCA-style plugs: three for the video and two for the audio.

• **Apple Composite AV Cable** This gives you three RCA-style plugs: one for the video and two for the audio.

These accessories need to be purchased individually from Apple. Many third-party manufacturers make cheaper versions, which should work with the iPad, assuming they have the appropriate Dock connector, though it's always worth checking with the manufacturer before you buy, as some may only work with older iOS devices.

AirPlay and screen mirroring

AirPlay is an Apple technology that allows you to stream content from an iPad to an Apple TV, connected via an HDMI cable to either a TV set or projector. To get this working while using the Videos app (or any other AirPlay enabled app), tap the ⬛ icon to switch playback between your iPad's screen and an Apple TV on the same Wi-Fi network.

If you have a second- or third-gen iPad, it is possible to "mirror" whatever you happen to have on your iPad's screen at any one time to an Apple TV – even if the application in question is not specifically AirPlay-enabled. This is great for everything from playing iPad games on a bigger screen to quickly zapping a webpage to the TV so that the whole family can see it. To start mirroring, double-tap the Home button to reveal the Multitasking Bar and then swipe to the right so that you can see the player controls. Next tap the ⬛ icon, choose the Apple TV you want to stream to and then slide the Mirroring switch to the **On** position. To find out more about Apple TV, visit apple. com/appletv.

YouTube

The iPad comes with a dedicated YouTube app, which can be used to access all the content from YouTube (assuming you are connected to the internet). Once a clip is playing, tap to see the onscreen playback controls. They work in exactly the same way as the video controls in the Videos app (see p.183), though here you can additionally:

• **Create Favorites** Tap the **Add** button to add a video clip to your **Favorites** list (accessed via the tab at the bottom).

• **Share clips** Tap the **Share** buttton to send a link by email, add a clip to your **Favorites**, or share it in a Tweet.

You can also sign in using a YouTube account login (Google account logins also work) allowing you to access your uploads, subscriptions, Favorites, and also:

• **Leave feedback** Tap the **Like** and **Dislike** buttons at the top of the clip window or **Flag** (if you find the clip offensive).

• **Create playlists** Tap **More** > **Playlists** to edit, create and delete YouTube playlists.

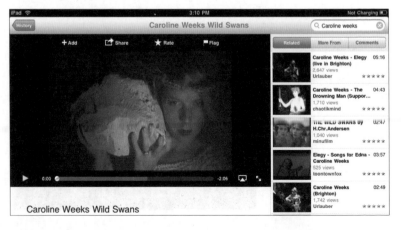

18

Apps: TV & video

Streaming TV and alternate video player apps

The video apps built-in to the iPad are all well and good, but they don't give you any options yet for watching live TV or for dealing with many of the common video file formats that you might have lurking on your computer. The Entertainment category of the App Store is the place to look for the necessary tools. Here are our recommendations.

Streaming live and catch-up TV

The main limitations to watching either live or catch-up TV on the iPad are regional: many services that are currently accessible in Europe aren't in the US, and vice versa. You are sure to find some that work, but don't be too surprised if a few of the apps listed below dish you up a whole lot of nothing.

BBC iPlayer

It took the BBC a while to get around to launching this catch-up (and live) TV and radio player app, but we are glad they did. The app allows you to stream content over both cellular data and Wi-Fi connections, though do keep your data plan in mind if you get addicted to the cellular feed.

TVCatchup

This app is the only thing you need to stream live UK Freeview TV to the iPad (though you do have to put up with an advert at the start of each session). It isn't great over a cellular data connection, but works very well over Wi-Fi.

Boxee

Boxee are one of the big names in web-based streaming TV services and set-top box systems. As well as all the online channels that this app gives you, you can also use it to stream any video format from your networked computer ... particularly handy where you have formats that otherwise won't work with iTunes and the iPad's Videos app. For the latest news about the Boxee service, visit boxee.tv.

Netflix

Subscribe to the Netflix service and get unlimited access to their library of TV series and movies. There's plenty of great stuff, but the new release selection isn't that current – for that, go to the LOVEFiLM Player app.

Hulu Plus

This app gives you access to the popular US subscription service. Loads of the major networks are covered, with season passes, 720p HD offerings and tools for managing your play queue.

Other video players

The biggest limitation of the iPad when it comes to video playback is the formats that are supported by the Videos app. Thankfully, there are several apps that offer an alternative:

GoodPlayer

Great all-round video player for the iPad that can handle pretty much any file format (Xvid, Divx, MKV, MP4, etc).

ProPlayer

Another good option that can handle all manner of files. Additionally, ProPlayer has loads of other features and tools for organizing and playing your files.

Plex

If you use the excellent Plex media server service to make your music, video and photos available for personal use across the web, then check out their iOS app to get access

Recording from TV

If you want to create iPad-friendly videos by recording from television, your best bet is to use a TV receiver for your computer.

Hauppauge, Freecom and others produce USB products for PCs. Browse Amazon or another major technology retailer to see what's on offer.

The obvious choice for Mac users is Elgato's superb EyeTV range of portable TV receivers, some of which are as small as a box of matches. You can either connect one to a proper TV aerial or, in areas of strong signal, just attach the tiny aerial that comes with the device. The most interesting piece of hardware for iPad owners is the Netstream DTT and Netstream Sat TV tuners, which both connect wirelessly to the Elgato EyeTV Netstream app, giving you live TV from a regular TV source direct to your iPad. For more info, see: elgato.com from your iPad or iPhone. To get the system up and running you will also need the Plex Media Server running on your desktop machine at home. Find out more at www.plexapp.com.

Listings & info

TV Guide Mobile
This US app is one of many TV-guide apps that can be found in the Store. It displays channels based on zip code and regional provider settings and has a nice user interface. In the UK a good equivalent is entitled TV Guide and comes with different screen views depending on whether you use it in portrait or landscape mode.

IMDb
This popular online source for movie and TV information is now in app form – an absolutely essential download.

Movies by Flixster
One-stop-shop for all your cinema needs: localized show times, trailers and reviews from Rotten Tomatoes.

Zeebox
This TV guide also acts as a real-time social networking tool for TV addicts. Sign in with either your Twitter or Facebook credentials and follow the tweets and posts of other viewers watching the same shows as you, as you watch.

Reading

19

iBooks

Apple's eBook reader and store

For many, the primary reason for buying an iPad is to use it as an eBook reader, and Apple are very much hoping that you will use their iBooks app to do just that, simultaneously giving you access to the Apple iBookstore, from which you can download thousands of tomes at the touch of a button.

iBooks is not one of the default apps on the iPad. It is a free app, but you will have to visit the App Store to download it. Unfortunately, not every country has an iBookstore, so if you can't find the iBooks app in your local App Store, it means that you are going to have to find another way of getting books onto your iPad. (Skip forward to the next chapter to find the answer.)

Using the iBooks app

Once launched, iBooks displays either a pretty bookshelf (your Library) or the iBookstore (which looks very similar to the iPad's iTunes Store). To toggle between the two, tap the button in the top-left corner of the app. When viewing your bookshelf you can switch between views of **Books**, **PDFs**, or new categories of your own making by tapping the **Collections** button. Though you can't purchase PDFs from the iBookstore, they can be synced across from iTunes or moved to the app from an email attachment or a link in Safari.

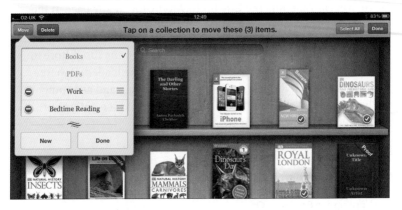

....

TIP You can toggle between the "bookshelf" and "list" views of your library using the two buttons on the top-right.

....

To change the position of a book on your shelf, tap and hold until it appears to lift, and then drag. To delete books or transfer them to a different **Collection**, tap **Edit**, then tap the item or items in question and then tap either **Move** or **Delete**.

....

TIP The version of the app that you install on the iPad features the ability to read fully illustrated titles that cannot be installed to the version of iBooks that runs on the iPhone and iPod touch.

....

Using the iBookstore

There aren't any surprises here. You browse and purchase books in just the same way that you do music, movies and TV shows in the iTunes Store. The iBookstore even uses exactly the same login credentials that you already use in the iTunes Store. You'll quickly get the hang of it.

• **Sample chapters** In most cases you can tap **Get Sample** to download a free excerpt to whet your appetite. You can download the full text at any time whilst reading (assuming you are connected to the internet) by tapping the **Buy** button at the top of any page in the sample.

• **Redownloading purchases** Tap **Purchases** in the iBookstore to see a list of all the books you have previously downloaded. If there are items in the list that are no longer on your iPad, and assuming the books are still available in the store, you should see options to **Redownload** them again for free.

> **TIP** If you want your book purchases from the iBookstore to automatically sync with your other iOS devices, look within the **Settings > Store** area on each and set the **Automatic Downloads** option for **Books** to **On**.

Reading fiction with iBooks

iBooks cleverly knows what kind of book you are reading, and adjusts the controls accordingly, depending on whether you are looking at heavily illustrated books or regular prose titles, such as novels or short stories.

To open a novel, or similar text-based book, tap it within your iBooks Library. It either opens to display a single-page view (in portrait mode)

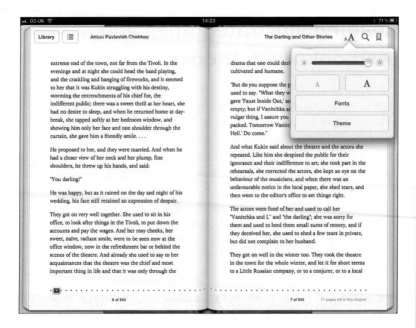

or a spread of two pages (in landscape mode). To turn a page, either drag the bottom corner, swipe across the screen, or tap to the left or right of the text near the edge of the iPad's screen.

A single tap anywhere on the body of the page will reveal or hide further options at the top and bottom, including text size and font options, brightness, night-reading and sepia modes (tap **Themes** to make your choice), a bookmark, and text search. It will also reveal a slider at the bottom of the page to help you quickly jump to another part of the book, either by tapping or dragging.

> **TIP** Look within **Settings > iBooks** to determine whether tapping on the left margin takes you to the next page or the previous page. Also note the options for text justification and hyphenation.

Reading illustrated titles and textbooks with iBooks

When reading illustrated iBooks titles on the iPad, the controls that appear when you tap the screen are slightly different, as you do not have an option to change the size of the text on the page, and there is an additional button for taking notes. This format allows publishers to add a wealth of additional functions and features, so expect to find your pages coming to life with embedded video, 3D models, galleries and interactive graphics.

Pinching across the pages of such titles reveals a preview gallery of all the book's pages at the bottom of the screen. Swipe left and right to zoom quickly through the previews and then tap to be taken directly to a given page.

Illustrated iBooks titles are generally read with the iPad held in landscape mode, but many also have a portrait "reader" mode, which presents the same material as a single flow of copy and images, more like the way iBooks handles fiction and prose titles. When reading like this, iBooks does, once more, give you back the option to change the font size via the toolbar controls at the top of the screen.

TIP If you are interested in creating your own illustrated eBook titles for the iBookstore and have a Mac running OS X Lion, then download the free iBooks Author software from the Mac Store, for which you'll find an icon on your Mac computer's Dock.

Other iBooks tricks

The following tools and functions work in both illustrated and prose iBooks titles.

• **Contents page** Tap the ≣ button to view the **Contents** page of the title you are reading; from there, tap **Resume** to return to the point where you were reading.

• **Dictionary** Tap and hold any word and choose **Define** from the options bubble to view a full definition (complete with derivatives and the word's origins).

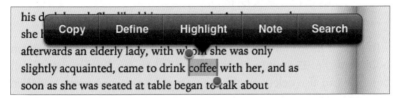

• **Search** Tap and hold any word and choose **Search** from the options bubble; this displays a tappable list of other places where the word occurs in the text and also offers two further links for searching the web and Wikipedia.

• **VoiceOver** iBooks supports Apple's VoiceOver screen reader, which will read the text aloud for you. Turn it on within **Settings** > **General** > **Accessibility**. The voice is a little mechanical, so you may decide you'd be better off with an audiobook (see p.171) or an iBooks title that comes with its own audio track built in (as is the case for many children's titles).

Adding Notes, Highlights and Bookmarks

Tap and hold the text you want to add a note or highlight to and then drag the blue anchor points to adjust the size of the selection, or simply drag across the text you want to highlight in illustrated titles. When you are ready, tap either **Highlight** or **Note** (and, in the latter case, start typing). Tapping margin notes and highlighted text again reveals options to change colours, change a highlight to an underline, and delete. To add a bookmark to a page (and you can have as many as you want), tap the 🔖 icon next to the search icon at the top.

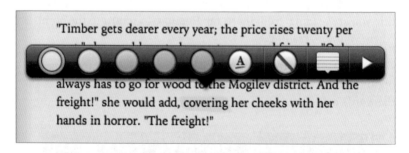

To view a list of all the highlights, notes and bookmarks in a given book, tap the ☰ button at the top, and then tap **Bookmarks**. From here you can also delete specific items from the list by swiping and then tapping **Delete**.

> **TIP** iBooks remembers where you are when you exit a book and will take you to the same point next time you open the title.

Reading PDFs with iBooks

When viewing a PDF sent as an attachment in an email or online within Safari, you should see an **Open in iBooks** button which will add the PDF to your iBooks library. Once this is done, the file will become available in the PDF section of your bookshelf – even when you are no longer connected to the internet.

The reader controls for PDFs are very similar to those for illustrated books. If you don't get on with iBooks as a PDF reader, try one of the alternative apps mentioned in the next chapter.

Deleting books and PDFs

To delete books from your iPad's Library, tap **Edit**, tap to select the titles you want to ditch, and then tap **Delete** to confirm. Books purchased from the iBookstore will still be available to sync back onto the iPad later for free via the **Purchased** tab.

You can build up a sizeable collection of eBook files on your iPad without having to worry about storage space. Text-only ePub books, even long ones, will only be a couple of megabytes at most (that's about the size of an average digital photo file); illustrated or interactive books and PDF documents, on the other hand, can be quite chunky.

> **TIP** To keep an eye on how much space books are taking up on your iPad, click **Settings > General > Usage** and look for the iBooks entry within the **Storage** list.

 iBooks
Version 2.0
App Size: 51.8 MB

Documents & Data   52.6 MB

Syncing with iTunes

To start syncing your books and PDF documents with iTunes, connect your iPad, select the **Books** tab, and then check the appropriate sync options. Note that you can choose to sync just books, just PDFs or both. Once this is set up, new iBookstore downloads and stored PDFs will be synced back to iTunes every time you connect, either via a cable or Wi-Fi.

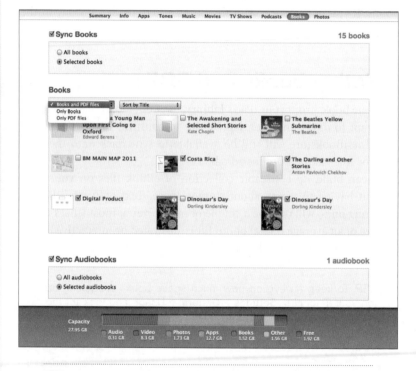

TIP This is also the panel within iTunes to visit if you want to sync audiobooks across from iTunes to your iPad. As an alternative source of audiobooks, check out the excellent Audible app (see p.206)

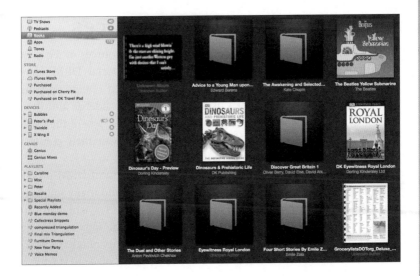

Even though you can't actually read your synced iBookstore purchases within iTunes on your computer, it's still a worthwhile exercise as a means of creating a backup of the titles you have downloaded. PDF files, on the other hand, can be dragged out of iTunes on your computer to be read onscreen.

Also, on your iPad, head to **Settings > iBooks** to set options for whether you want any Bookmarks or organized Collections to be synced back into iTunes along with the books themselves. And if you want new iBook purchases to automatically find their way on to both your computer and iPad, then make sure that Automatic Downloads is set up in both iTunes on your Mac or PC (see p.160) and on the iPad (see p.167).

> **TIP** If no Books listing appears under Library in the iTunes sidebar
> on your computer, open **iTunes Preferences** and check the **Books**
> box on the **General** pane.

ePub books from other sources

iBooks can also display "ePub" format books from sources other than the iBookstore (assuming they don't have any special DRM copy protection built in). First, you need to get them into iTunes on your computer. Highlight the **Books** listing in the iTunes sidebar and then drag and drop the files into the main iTunes window, where they will appear alongside your iBookstore purchases. You can then connect your iPad and sync them across in the normal way.

This won't work for ePub files that employ any form of DRM piracy controls (such as those from the Sony Reader Store and many publishers' sites). Neither will this work for Amazon Kindle files, which are an entirely different file format altogether and require the separate Kindle app to work on the iPad (see p.203). But there are plenty of other DRM-free ePub sources that you can turn to. One excellent place to start is:

ePubBooks epubbooks.com

Whether you are an author yourself, or a student, there are loads of benefits to being able to create your own standard prose ePub files. To give it a go, try:

Storyist storyist.com
eCub juliansmart.com/ecub

> **TIP** If you are looking for a way to read ePub files on your Mac or PC, try the free-to-use Adobe Digital Editions (adobe.com/products/digitaleditions).

20

Apps: Books

Readers, comics and kids' books

Using iBooks is not the only way to read eBooks on the iPad, as most of the main eBook sellers have their own dedicated apps. And when it comes to specialist graphic titles, such as comics and manga, you will not be disappointed when turning to the App Store to get your fix.

eBook reading apps

Kindle
For reading Amazon eBooks this a great little app and has a similar set of features to iBooks. You can't actually browse the Amazon store from within the app; for that you need to head to the website and then sync your purchases over the airwaves.

Stanza
This reader and store offer thousands of titles and you can add your own files using the Stanza Desktop application.

Google Play Books

Syncs via the cloud with your Google Books account and has a nice reader interface which, like Stanza and iBooks, includes a white-on-black night-reading mode. As with the Kindle app, you have to shop for titles outside the app on the associated website.

Kobo

A nice-looking app that gives you access to thousands of titles from the Kobo store. The reading experience is excellent, with font and bookmarking options. There is also a useful feature that lets you add titles via either an iCloud or Dropbox account.

Kids' reading apps

There is a glut of kids' content to be found in the App Store Books category, but do read the reviews and be selective, as the majority of what's there is shockingly poor. Here are a few that are worth a go:

Ladybird Classic Me Books

This beautiful reader app gives you access to the iconic Ladybird Me Books series. You get *The Zoo* for free, and then build your collection via in-app purchases. Many feature audio of the text read by famous names, and you can even record your own sound effects and narration as you read.

> **TIP** To stop your kids racking up a massive bill when using apps that feature in-app purchases, look to **Settings > General > Restrictions** to disable the **In-App Purchase** function.

Nursery Rhymes with StoryTime

One of a growing number of apps that strive to take the book/app hybrid format to the next level. With audio, moveable objects and delightful graphics, this is a treat for all ages and includes loads of classic favourite nursery rhymes. And best of all, mums and dads away from home can use the app to read to their little ones remotely – great when travelling on business.

The Cat in the Hat

Ingeniously adapted for the screen, you can read this like a book, listen to the narrative or play the whole thing through like a movie. Other Dr Seuss titles are also in the App Store.

Comics and graphic novels

Marvel

Access to an essential store of classic superhero comics – Spider-Man, Thor, Wolverine and Iron Man are all here, alongside a seemingly endless list of both very obscure and classic material. Download and read either page by page (as you would in a regular comic) or double-tap to read frame by frame.

Comics+

A really easy-to-use store and comic reader from iVerse. There are both paid-for and free comics to be found and downloaded here. Viewed in portrait mode, you get the original comic book pages, and, when turned to landscape mode, you see a special "adapted view" custom-created for the mobile screen.

TIP As well as all the "store" and "library" apps, there are also thousands of comics to be found published as standalone apps.

Miscellaneous

Audible

The iPad's Music app does a perfectly good job of playing back audiobook content purchased from the iTunes Store, but if you want a dedicated audiobook app, then this is the one to go for. The navigation and playback tools are excellent and you can also share your listening habits via Facebook and Twitter.

Bookscan for iBooks

Point your iPad's camera at the barcode on any "real" book, and this app will tell you whether the title is available in the iBookstore and present you with a link to get there.

Brilliant Quotes & Quotations

Though you can find similar titles in the App Store Reference section, this is one of the better put together collections. There are some nice sharing and Tweeting options, but it is the content that really speaks for itself.

21

Apps: News

Read all about it on the iPad

The iPad, with its integrated Newsstand feature, is ideally suited to delivering your daily fix of current affairs, or any other kind of news for that matter, wherever you want it, and in a perfectly digestible format. So, whether you read in bed, on the train, on the couch or at the breakfast table, there are apps that can act as a handy replacement for a newspaper or magazine.

Standalone news apps

Many of the major news and magazine publishers are battling to define their place in the digital marketplace. Some media have opted to make their apps free, but with advertising; some use subscription; others charge a one-time fee for users to download their app. The real question here is not whether you want to pay for news (there are still a thousand places online where the latest stories can be harvested for free), but whether you are prepared to pay for a particular stance, attitude or editorial voice – which is what we do in the real world when we choose to hand over cash for a print newspaper. Some recommendations:

BBC News

This app has a really nice user interface in both landscape and portrait modes, complete with a handy news-ticker that dishes up the latest headlines and embedded video content alongside the written news stories. You can customize the news categories that you want to see and share stories vie email, Facebook and Twitter.

The Wall Street Journal

Register for free to see the latest news presented in a beautiful format that successfully mimics the look of the print version. For full access to various sections of the paper you need to buy in-app subscriptions.

Newsstand

Tap the Newsstand app icon on your Home Screen to get quick access to subscription magazine and news services that publish into the Newsstand category of the App Store, but without the hussle and bustle of the regular News category. To furnish your Newsstand with publications, either browse via the App Store or tap the shortcut button at the top of the expanded Newsstand panel. In most cases, you can then subscribe or purchase new issues from within each publication and get notifications when new publications are made available.

USA Today

Neat interface with an easy-to-navigate layout. Scrolling from page to page in long articles is particularly well handled, and the embedded video clips are an added bonus.

Longform

An impressive magazine-style curated reading experience, Longform is worth taking for a spin if you want to get a cross-section of articles and news from across the world of media, but without having to do all the hard work of subscribing to feeds and the like.

> **TIP** The Financial Times no longer has a dedicated app in the App Store; instead you need to visit their excellent web app (app. ft.com). It is free to browse a small amount of teaser content, but you have to sign up for a subscription to get the full package.

News aggregators

Many news apps use RSS – Really Simple Syndication – to pull "feeds" or "newsfeeds" from blogs, news services and other websites. Each feed consists of images, headlines and summaries or full articles. At the time of writing, arguably the best web-based aggregator service is Google Reader, which can be set up via reader.google.com, using the same credentials you use for other Google services.

As for dedicated apps for reading your aggregated newsfeeds, try one of these, all of which make varied and interesting visual use of the iPad's screen real estate:

Early Edition 2
This iPad-only aggregator creates a dynamic custom layout based on the feeds you point it at. It feels like a newspaper to read, and has some very nice extras, such as a gallery mode that pulls together all of the images associated with your stories.

Pulse
One of the more beautiful news aggregator apps, Pulse pulls together newsfeeds from multiple sites and integrates with Google Reader to create a mosaic of content that is easy and fun to digest.

NewsRack
Offline viewing, Google Reader integration and a well-designed interface make this app a solid reader choice.

Flipboard
The very popular Flipboard pulls together news, website feeds and social media feeds (from Facebook and Twitter, say) to create a very stylish, personalized magazine-like experience.

The
internet

22

Safari

The iPad's web browser

The iPad comes with a version of the Safari web browser. Anyone who has ever used Safari on the iPhone or iPod touch will feel very at home, while the extra screen size and speedy processing power of the iPad take things to another level. It can't do everything – Flash (a technology used for online video and animation) doesn't display – but Safari is still an impressive browser experience.

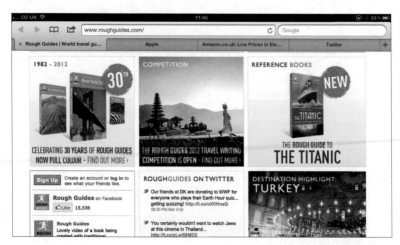

The basics

Make sure you have either a Wi-Fi or cellular data signal, as discussed in the Connecting chapter, and then tap **Safari** on the Home Screen.

• **Enter an address** Tap into the address field at the top of the screen; tap ✖ to clear the current address and start typing. Note the ".com" key for quickly completing addresses. Then tap **Go**.

> **TIP** If you tap and hold the ".com" key, other common web address suffixes appear: ".net", ".org", ".co.uk", etc.

• **Search the web** Tap into the search field at the top of the screen and start typing. When you're done, hit **Search**. You can select any of the suggested search items that appear while you're typing.

> **TIP** If you want to switch from Google (the default) to Yahoo! or Bing searching, look within **Settings > Safari > Search Engine**. Of course, you can also visit any search engine by typing in its address and then use it in the normal way.

• **Search the current page** As you type into the search field, also note that below the list of suggested web search results there is a link for viewing search results found on the currently loaded page. Tap this and then use the ◀ and ▶ buttons to skip between the various instances of the phrase or word.

• **Reload/refresh** If a page hasn't loaded properly, or you want to make sure you're viewing the latest version of the page, click ↻.

• **To follow a link** Tap once. If you did it by accident, press ◀.

> **TIP** You can see the full URL of any link by tapping and holding the relevant text or image. (This is equivalent to hovering over a link with a mouse using a desktop web browser.)

• **To share a page's address** When viewing a page, tap the ↱ icon and then tap **Mail Link to this Page**. A new email will appear with the link in the body and the webpage's title in the subject line. You can also tap **Tweet** to publish the address to Twitter. For this to work you must first enter your Twitter account details within **Settings > Twitter**.

• **Zoom** Double-tap on any part of a page – a column, headline or picture, say – to zoom in on it or to zoom back out. Alternatively, "pinch out" with your finger and thumb (or any two digits of your choice). Once zoomed, you can drag the page around with one finger.

• **Scroll** You can use your fingers to scroll up, down or sideways in Safari on the iPad. One finger scrolls the entire page, two fingers will scroll within a specific frame of a webpage.

> **TIP** Having scrolled down a long page, quickly get back to the top by tapping the clock display on the iPad's Status Bar at the top.

• **To open a page in Reader view** Reader view gives you a clean, ad-free text-and-pictures version of the current page, allowing you to read articles and posts in a more digestible iPad-friendly format. There is even a link at the top of the page to change the text size (like in iBooks). If Reader view is available for the page you are looking at, a button will appear in the address field at the top.

Tabbed browsing

Just like browsers on a Mac or PC, Safari on the iPad can handle multiple pages at once in the form of tabs. These are especially useful when you're struggling with a slow connection, and you don't want to close a page that you may want to come back to later.

• **Open a new tab** Tap the ✚ to the right of the open tab headers to open a blank tab. To open a web link into a new tab, hold the link; then choose **Open in New Tab** from the option bubble. To ensure that new tabs open behind the one you are currently viewing, look for the option within **Settings** > **Safari** > **General**.

• **Switch between tabs** Tap any of the tab headers.

• **Change the order of open tabs** Tap any tab header and drag it to the left or right to shuffle its position.

• **Close a tab** Tap the ✖ on the left edge of a tab header.

Webpage display problems

If a webpage looks weird on screen – bad spacing, images overlapping, etc – there are two likely causes. First, it could be that the page isn't properly "web compliant". That is, it looked okay on the browser on which the designer tested it (Internet Explorer, for example), but doesn't display properly on other browsers (such as Safari on the iPad).

Second, it could be that the page includes elements based on technologies that the iPad doesn't handle, such as Adobe Flash. This is especially likely to be the problem if there's a gap in an otherwise normal page, though sometimes Safari closes such gaps where there should be Flash, which can play havoc with the page's intended layout.

If a webpage looks okay, but different from the version you're used to seeing on your Mac or PC, it could be that the website in question has been set up to detect your browser and automatically offer you a small-screen version.

Bookmarks

Bookmarks, like Home Screen web-clips (see p.72), are always handy, but when using a device without a mouse and keyboard, they're even handier than usual. To bookmark a page to return to later on the iPad, tap ⤴ and then **Add Bookmark**. To retrieve a bookmark, tap ⊞, browse and then click the relevant entry. To edit your bookmarks…

• **To delete a bookmark or folder** Tap **Edit** at the top of the panel followed by the relevant ⊖ icon. Hit **Delete** to confirm.

• **To edit a bookmark or folder** Tap **Edit**, hit the relevant entry, and then type into the name and URL fields.

• **To create a new folder** Tap **Edit**, then **New Folder**.

• **To move a bookmark or folder** Tap **Edit** and slide it up or down using the ☰ icon. Alternatively, tap **Edit**, then hit the relevant entry and use the lower field to pick the folder into which you'd like to move the bookmark or folder.

> **TIP** The Bookmarks button ⊞ also gives you access to your Safari **Reading List**, where you can store links to articles or webpages you might want to come back to and read later (but not keep for posterity as you might Bookmarks). When you come across a webpage you'd like to read later, tap the ⤴ button and choose **Add to Reading List**.

Syncing bookmarks from your Mac or PC

Using iCloud

The easiest way to sync your bookmarks with Safari on either a Mac or PC, or with Internet Explorer on a PC, is via iCloud. To check that bookmarks are set to sync, look within **Settings > iCloud** on your iPad. Then, on a Mac, go to **System Preference > iCloud,** and, on a PC, launch the iCloud Control Panel (Icloud.com/icloudcontrolpanel) to check that the sync is set up from that end. iCloud also syncs your Reading List along with Bookmarks. And with iCloud enabled on other iOS devices as well as your iPad, everything will be synced there too.

Using iTunes

You can also sync bookmarks via iTunes. Just connect your iPad (either wirelessly or via a cable) and click its icon in iTunes. Click the **Info** tab and check the relevant box under **Other**. The bookmarks will move across to the iPad once you have hit **Apply** and then **Sync**.

> **TIP** Use the free Xmarks service (xmarks.com) to sync other browsers' bookmarks to Safari, and in turn the iPad.

Forms and AutoFill

You can set Safari on the iPad to remember the names and passwords that you use frequently on websites, though if you do, there is a risk that someone else could use those credentials on a website if they got hold of your iPad. You can turn the feature on or off within **Settings > Safari > AutoFill** – look for the option to turn on **Names & Passwords**. If you do enable it, make sure you've also set a four-digit security code to unlock the iPad's Lock Screen. This is found within **Settings > General > Passcode Lock**.

AutoFill can also help you when filling out address fields on webpages, though you will need to tell the iPad which contact details to use for this. First enable AutoFill, as already described, and then turn on **Use Contact Info**, choose **My Info** and select your contact entry from your iPad's **Contacts** list. If at any time you wish to remove all the saved passwords and usernames on your iPad, tap **Clear All**.

Safari settings

You'll find various browsing preferences under **Settings > Safari**. Here you can empty your cache and history (useful if Safari keeps crashing, or you want to hide your tracks), play with security settings (make sure that the **Fraud Warning** option is switched on), choose a search engine, turn the **Bookmarks Bar** on and off, and also access options for the following:

• **Private Browsing** With this turned on, your Safari activity will not generate any stored browsing history nor add any new entries to your AutoFill data.

• **JavaScript** This is a ubiquitous way to add extra functions to websites and is best left on.

• **Pop-up blocker** Stops pop-up pages (mainly ads) from opening.

• **Cookies and data** Cookies are files that websites save on your iPad to enable content and preferences tailored for you, for example, specific recommendations on a shopping site. To delete all this data, tap the **Clear Cookies and Data** button. Alternatively, tap through to the **Advanced > Website Data** screen to see exactly how much data specific sites are saving to your iPad. From here you can tap **Edit** and then delete the cached data for specific sites if you so wish.

History and cache

Like most browsers, Safari on the iPad stores a list of all the websites you visit. These allow the iPad to offer suggestions when you're typing an address but can also be browsed – useful if you need to find a site for the second time but can't remember its address. To browse your history, look at the top of your Bookmarks list, accessible at any time via the ⬚ icon. To clear your history, look for the option in **Settings** > **Safari**.

Unfortunately, despite storing your history, Safari doesn't "cache" (temporarily save) each page you visit in any useful way. This is a shame, as it means you can't quickly visit a bunch of pages for browsing when you're offline. It also explains why using the ◀ button is slower on the iPad than on a computer – when you click ◀, you download the page in question afresh rather than returning to a cached version.

Viewing PDFs and Word documents

The iPad can view Word, Excel and PDF documents on the web, creating an iPad-friendly preview version in a popover window. Once opened, scroll down to read subsequent pages, and double-tap to zoom in just as you would with a regular webpage.

In the case of PDFs, assuming you have the free Apple iBooks app installed, look out for the ↱ button to then **Open in iBooks** (tap the screen once if you don't see it). This link will save a copy of the PDF to your iBooks bookshelf. The file is then moved back to iTunes next time you sync either wirelessly or via a cable.

If you use a different PDF reading app, such as GoodReader (see p.32), or want to move the PDF to a file storage app (such as Dropbox, see p.247), tap the **Open in...** link and choose your app from the list.

> **TIP** If you're following a link from Google to a PDF, Word or Excel doc, and it is taking an age to download, click the **View As HTML** link instead of the main link to the document. This way you'll get a faster-loading text-only version.

iPad Googling tips

The search field at the top of every Safari page on the iPad is an incredibly useful tool and, as you start to type, its dynamic popover list of suggested searches makes it even more so. What's more, Google's results page is optimized for the iPad, with links at the top for jumping between different search types – "web", "images", and so on.

All the following tricks work on both a PC and Mac as well as an iPad. Typing the text as shown here in bold will yield the following search results:

Basic searches

william lawes > the terms "william" and "lawes"

"william lawes" > the phrase "william lawes"

william OR lawes > either "william" or "lawes" or both

william -lawes > "william" but not "lawes".

All these commands can be mixed and doubled up. Hence:

"william lawes" OR "will lawes" -composer > either version of the name but not the word "composer".

Synonyms

~mac > "mac" and related words, such as "Apple" and "Macintosh".

Definitions

define:calabash > definitions from various sources for the word "calabash". You can also get definitions of a search term by clicking the definitions link at the right-hand end of the top blue strip on the results page.

Flexible phrases

"william * lawes" > "william john lawes", etc, as well as just "william lawes".

Search within a specific site

site:bbc.co.uk "jimmy white" > pages containing Jimmy White's name within the BBC website. This is often far more effective than using a site's internal search.

Search web addresses

"arms exports" inurl:gov > the phrase "arms exports" in the webpages with the term gov in the address (i.e. government websites).

Search page titles

train bristol in title:timetable > pages with "timetable" in their titles, and "train" and "bristol" anywhere in the page.

Number and price ranges

1972..1975 "snooker champions" > the term "snooker champions" and any number (or date) in the range 1972–1975.

$15..$30 "snooker cue" > the term "snooker cue" and any price that falls in the range $15–30.

Search specific file types

filetype:pdf climate change statistics > would find PDF documents (likely to be more "serious" reports than webpages) containing the terms "climate", "change" and "statistics".

Searching without your keyboard

To search the web without even typing, head to the App Store and download the Google Search app, which allows you to search not only by talking (Voice Search), but also by pointing your iPad's camera at something you want to know about (Google Goggles) or based on where you are (My Location).

23

Apps for the web

Other ways to surf and browse

There are several alternative browsers available in the App Store, but none that offers all the features and integration of Safari (see p.212). Browse or search both the Utilities and Productivity categories to see what's available, or try one of these:

Web browsers

Opera Mini
From the same people who make the brilliant desktop Opera browser, this iPad version is impressively fast and features tabbed browsing, password tools and a very slick quick access "Speed Dial" tool to get you to your favourite sites.

VanillaSurf

If you're not satisfied by Safari's tabbed browsing feature, this is the app to download for a very impressive, full-screen alternative tabbed browsing fix. It has tons of nice extra features, including a downloads manager, offline browsing and book-mark syncing. (For offline reading, also try the reader apps reviewed on p.224.)

Skyfire

Another excellent alternative to Safari, this time with the addition of multiple user support (great if different people in your family want their own settings and bookmarks) and also support for Flash video (though not flash animations and games, at the time of writing).

Mercury Web Browser

Another very handy Safari alternative. This one can be decorated with themes, features Firefox syncing tools and Dropbox integration, and has various finger gestures for swift browsing.

FREE Full Screen Private Browsing for iPhone & iPad

A no-frills affair that offers completely private browsing sessions: no history, no cache, no cookies. Though you can achieve the same thing by enabling the function for Safari (**Settings > Safari > Private Browsing**), you might find it easier to have a separate app available that always behaves in this way. Catchy app name too.

Duo Browser

One of several browsers in the App Store that give you the functionality to browse two sites simultaneously on the same screen in a split view.

Reading webpages later

As mentioned in the previous chapter, the Reading List feature (see p.216) built into Safari is worth taking a look at. There are also several apps that perform a similar task. Though not all websites will work with such services, enough do that they are worthwhile playing around with:

Instapaper

If you don't get on with Apple's Reading List, sign up for the excellent Instapaper service (instapaper.com). The app has a really easy-on-the-eye, stripped-back feel; many RSS services integrate with it, as does Twitter, so you can have all your reading matter and stories with you, and available offline (assuming you remember to sync your app and Instapaper account before you disconnect from the internet).

Read It Later

This excellent bookmarking app has a really clean interface. The Pro version includes a very useful Bookmarklet (a special piece of JavaScript code) that allows you to quickly add pages and articles to your list straight from Safari on your iPad.

Visual Bookmarks

As the name suggests, this app gives you a very visual way to browse all your favourite links as a grid of webpage previews; it's a little like browsing albums in the Photos app.

Thumbs

Another visually striking grid-like bookmarking tool, this time with some nice customization options and the ability to tap to refresh the page preview.

24

Staying safe online

Avoiding hackers and scammers

The internet may be the greatest wonder of the modern world, but it does come with certain downsides. Increased access to information is great, but not if the information other people are accessing is yours – and private. Though Apple products are generally very secure, it's still worth remembering a few golden rules.

Protect yourself

If you want to keep your iPad, your files, and your private data safe, read the next couple of pages and make sure that you check all the boxes.

• **Keep your system up to date** Many security breaches involve a programmer taking advantage of a security flaw in your software, so it's critical to keep your iPad up to speed with the latest firmware updates. You should be prompted automatically when updates are available, but you can check for yourself by going to **Settings** > **General** > **Software Update** on your iPad; or, when connected to your computer via iTunes, click **Check for Updates** under the **Summary** tab.

• **Don't run dodgy software** Apple work hard to ensure that all the software that they make available in the App Store will be "clean" of viruses and other dangers. However, if you're offered any alternative routes to getting software onto your iPad, such as jailbreaking, steer clear … it's not worth the risk.

• **Hide behind a firewall** A firewall serves to prevent anyone from being able to find your computer, iPad or other devices on the internet, let alone invade it. If you use a wireless router at home, then you may well find that it has its own firewall. Make sure it's enabled and your iPad will be undetectable from the internet when connected via Wi-Fi.

• **Enable wireless security** Also, be sure to implement a few basic security measures to secure your domestic Wi-Fi network. First, add a WPA or WPA2 password (the older WEP standard just doesn't cut it these days) to make sure your connection is only used by the people you want to use it. Next, make sure you set a username and password for accessing your router settings (and make sure it's different to your Wi-Fi network's WPA password).

• **Don't respond to spam** Those "get paid to surf", "stock tips", "recruit new members", "clear your credit rating" and various network-marketing schemes are always too good to be true.

> **TIP** Also beware of "phishermen" trying to snag your bank details and passwords. For more, see p114.

• **Be careful of "adult" sites** It is often said that the majority of online scams involve porn sites – the scammers believing, probably correctly, that the victims will be too embarrassed to report the problem. If you do ever use an adult site, never pass over credit card details unless you're prepared to get stung. And, whatever you do, don't download any software they offer.

Security on the road

Next, here's a few golden rules to help keep your iPad secure away from home, and particularly when connected to public Wi-Fi networks.

• **Always use a screen lock** Make sure you're using a passcode-protected screen lock so that, should your machine be lost or stolen, its data will be inaccessible. Look in **Settings > General > Passcode Lock**. Also turn on the **Erase Data** function so that all your iPad's content is wiped after ten failed passcode attempts.

• **Avoid using banking sites out and about** If you use Wi-Fi hotspots, avoid accessing your bank accounts and any other sensitive material, as public networks are notorious for so-called "snoop" or "sidejacking" attacks, where data is intercepted by other machines using the same network. Where possible limit your activities to browsing that isn't security-sensitive. And always try to shield your keystrokes when entering passwords, just as you would with your PIN at an ATM.

Find My iPad

The "Find My iPad" feature can be used remotely to track the location of your iPad, add a four-digit passcode screen lock and even wipe all its content remotely – all very useful should it go astray. If you are using iCloud (see p.18), go to **Settings > iCloud** to set this up.

You can then visit the iCloud.com website on your computer and sign in using your Apple ID to be able to track the location of your iPad. Assuming the iPad is connected to either a Wi-Fi or cellular network at the time, you should be able to get a fix.

TIP There is also a Find My iPhone app that can be installed on any Apple iOS device, allowing you to track your iPad from another iPad, iPhone or iPod touch.

Passwords & AutoFill

Though obvious, there are a few basic ground rules worth reiterating here to make sure that your online identity remains secure – from online criminals, but also from members of your household who might inadvertently use your logins. In terms of Safari, it's worth treating your iPad just as you would a public machine and making sure that its AutoFill feature doesn't remember your passwords and login details by default as you browse (**Settings > Safari > AutoFill > Names and Passwords**). If you do choose to enable AutoFill, make sure you have a Passcode Lock set (see p.69). As for actual passwords:

• **Make them "strong"** It really should go without saying that you shouldn't use the word "password" as a password. Neither should you opt for pets' or family members' names. Instead, go for something with both letters and numbers, upper and lower case, and preferably that makes no sense at all.

• **Use multiple passwords** Create separate passwords for different logins on different sites. That way, if the password you use on one site is compromised, there is no danger that it can be used for any other sites. If this sounds like way too much to have to remember, come up with a secret formula – perhaps using the same basic root for all your passwords and then adding the initials of a given website's name.

• **Change them regularly** Again, this might sound like time that could be spent doing something less boring instead, but get into the habit of refreshing your passwords on a regular basis.

Secure your connections

Whenever entering sensitive data (passwords, usernames and the like) into a webpage, make sure that either a padlock icon appears on the tab title strip, or that the URL in the address field begins "https://" rather than simply "http://". The "s" signifies a secure connection that uses the so-called SSL (Secure Sockets Layer) or newer TLS (Transport Layer Security) protocols. If you are at all unsure about the security provided by a specific site or service, ask them for some clarity or use a different service.

TIP If you can't see http:// or https:// in the browser, tap on the address bar to see the full URL.

Password managers

A password manager is basically a piece of software that stores all your login details within an encrypted database on your iPad. Safari does have the AutoFill feature mentioned earlier, though when enabled, it gives everyone who uses your iPad access to your logins, which might be a problem if you have a communally used device.

There are also third-party password managers out there for the iPad. The best of the bunch is 1Password Pro, though it does still have its limitations. The main problem is that it doesn't integrate with Safari on the iPad, so to take advantage of its login tools, you need to browse the sites in question using the integrated browser – only really worth doing for particularly sensitive sites.

Restrictions

Finally, a note on the iPad's parental control features, which can be employed to stop users accessing Safari, YouTube, the iTunes and App Stores, location services, the dictation tool and more.

You can also prevent "in-app" purchases, set the amount of time your store password is available for once entered, and also set content-specific age limits for music, movies, TV shows and apps. You'll find the various options in **Settings > General > Restrictions**, where you also get to set a passcode to gain access to the quarantined activities and features.

Navigation & travel

25
Maps
Search and directions

The Maps app on the iPad takes you into the world of Google Maps, where you can quickly find locations, get directions and view satellite photos. You can zoom and scroll around the maps in the same way you would with webpages in Safari. You will need either a cellular or Wi-Fi internet connection active to see the mapping (as the maps are downloaded on the fly from Google's servers), so do keep that in mind before you head out on the road.

Searching for your current location

Any 3G or 4G iPad can accurately determine your current location by using a combination of data from its GPS (Global Positioning System) chip, a connected cellular network and also from a connected Wi-Fi network. The Wi-Fi-only iPad, on the other hand, has only got Wi-Fi to go on, so it needs to be connected to a network to be able to determine your location. Tap the ◢ icon at the top of the screen to determine your current location.

To find out which way you are facing, hold the iPad flat and tap the ◢ button for a second time; the app switches mode, allowing you to view the map in relation to the way you are facing. The narrower the white misty direction indicator coming out of your blue location marker, the more accurate the direction reading (as pictured).

Searching for a location

Tap the Search box and type a city, town or region, place of interest, or a ZIP or postcode. You can also try to find a business in the area you are viewing by entering either the name of the business or something more general – such as "camera", "hotel", or "pizza". Note, however, that the results, which are pulled from Google Local, won't be anything like comprehensive.

Location Services settings

Whenever the app you are currently using is hooked into Location Services (via either GPS, Wi-Fi or the cellular network) a dart ◢ icon appears in the Status Bar at the top of the iPad's screen. Look within **Settings** > **Location Services** to turn your iPad's location functionality on and off for either specific apps or everything. This can be a useful means of saving battery power. You can also see here which apps have used the iPad's Location Services in the last 24 hours as they display a purple ◢ icon.

Search results appear as a little red pin. If a multitude of pins appears, tap the ⊜ icon to see a popover panel of all the listings, which can then be tapped to identify them on the map. Alternatively, tap on each of the pins in turn to see its name. Tap a pin's blue ⓘ icon for further options, such as adding the location as a bookmark or contact address, emailing a link to the location or getting directions to or from that location.

> **TIP** In some areas you will also see a little orange ⬤ icon on a pin's popover panel. Tap this to scroll around in Google's Street View. When you're done, tap the inset map preview to finish.

Dropping pins

You can drop a pin manually at any time by tapping the page-curl, bottom-right, and then **Drop Pin**. This can be a handy way in which to keep your bearings when sliding around a map. To change the position of a pin, tap and hold it, then drag. To delete the pin or perform any of the functions listed above, tap the pin and then the ⓘ icon. Your lists of bookmarks and recently viewed locations can be viewed by tapping the ⊞ icon at the top.

> **TIP** The page-curl button also gives you access to a useful link for printing your current map view to any AirPrint-enabled printers (see p.248) on the same network as your iPad.

Satellite and Terrain views

Tapping the page-curl button reveals options to view **Satellite** images (they're not live, unfortunately … maybe one day), a **Hybrid** view that adds roads and labels from the **Standard** view to a satellite image, and also a **Terrain** view, which is nice, but doesn't allow you to zoom in as far as on the **Standard** view.

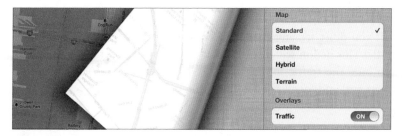

Directions

To view directions from one location to another, tap **Directions** at the top of the screen and enter start and end points, either by typing search terms or by tapping ⌕ to browse for bookmarks, addresses from your contacts or recently viewed items. Use the blue panel to choose between directions for driving, walking or taking public transport.

Once a journey is displaying, you can go through it one step at a time by tapping **Start** and using the arrow buttons to jump forward and back one stage. Also note the ▤ button, which shows your journey as a list of stages. When looking at directions for public transport routes, use the ◉ button to view a panel of transit times and schedules or tap on individual points along the route to get more detail about the changes you need to make.

> **TIP** For your return journey, reverse the directions displayed on your iPad by tapping the ⇄ button between the start and end-point fields.

Traffic conditions

In areas where the service is available, your route will display colour-coded information about traffic conditions:

- **Grey** No data currently available.
- **Red** Traffic moving at less than 25 miles per hour.
- **Yellow** Traffic moving at 25–50 miles per hour.
- **Green** Traffic moving at more than 50 miles per hour.

If you don't see any change in colour, you may need to zoom out a little. This action will also automatically refresh the traffic speed data. To hide the traffic information (perhaps you like surprises), tap the map-curl and toggle the **Traffic** button off.

Searching for other people

Putting aside for one moment issues of personal space and privacy, devices such as the iPad are now making it possible for you to geolocate your friends and family as and when you need to. Great for trying to meet up with people on a busy street; not so great if you told your other half that you were working late, when you're actually in a bar having, erm, another half!

Find my Friends

Apple's service requires you to download the app from the App Store and then invite friends to either "follow" you or see your location temporarily. You can also choose to make your location private as and when you need to.

Google Latitude

Google have an almost identical service, also with an app (optimized for iPhone) available in the App Store.

26

Apps: navigation & travel

The best map and location tools

The App Store has separate categories dedicated to Navigation and Travel, where you'll find everything from plane and ship location tools to multifunctional compass applications. Here are a few of the best.

FlightTrack

This app is a revelation for frequent flyers. It gives you all the live flight info you could wish for, syncs your bookmarked flights to your calendar and can be used to track the status of any flight, either on the ground or in the air, on a map. You can also overlay a weather feed to see where your ride might get a little bumpy, and there's even an offline mode that you can use whilst in the air.

Google Earth

An essential free app that gives you unfettered access to the globe. When you swipe with two fingers, or alter the tilt of your iPad, you adjust the pitch of your view, which allows you to achieve some amazing vistas of mountainous regions. It can feel quite clunky at times, especially over a slow connection, as the higher resolution views can take a while to load, but it is worth being patient.

GPS Navigation 2

Pulling its information from the OpenStreetMap project, this voice-guided turn-by-turn navigation system really is ahead of the curve. Buy the app once and then download individual area data sets (Europe, UK, etc) at very reasonable prices.

Jetsetter

In contrast to the clutter of most online hotel booking experiences, this app is all about presenting the best hotels within a sumptuous and uncluttered digital arena. With 360-degree panoramas, loads of photography and reviews, this app makes picking your hotel almost as fun as actually being there.

Map+

Create your own custom maps using the built-in set of colourful and varied pins and icons. You can usefully attach notes, addresses and photos to individual points of interest.

Maplets

Great collection of offline national park and bike trail maps for both the US and international destinations. There are also hundreds of ski maps and transport maps available to download and use later when you don't have access to the internet.

Peakfinder Alps

To be used either on location or not, Peakfinder pulls together extraordinary 360-degree panoramas of all the peaks in the Alps. There is a binocular zoom mode for distant peaks and digital compass integration. Similar Peakfinder apps also exist for mountains in the US and Canada.

Pin Drop

Falling somewhere between a social network and a constantly evolving personalized travel guide, this app lets you bookmark locations, view others' pins, and much more.

Plane Finder AR

This extraordinary app allows you to point your iPad at any plane in the sky to find out information about it. (The AR of the app's name stands for "augmented reality".) The same company also make a Ship Finder AR app.

Skyscanner

Great app for finding the cheapest flights. It searches across nearly all the airlines and re-sellers and serves up the results in an easily digestible form.

Spyglass – AR Compass

This augmented reality toolkit works brilliantly on the iPad's screen: its AR mode layers the compass readout over the camera's view. The integrated Gyrocompass is also impressive.

TrakPal Lite

Nice heads-up display that shows your current altitude, direction speed and acceleration.

Tripit

Useful app that aggregates all your trip information (flights, transfers, hotel bookings, etc) into one place. The paid app comes without ads, while the addition of a Pro account gives you live flight updates amongst other perks.

Transit Maps

Use this app to locate, download and store transit maps from around the world that you can then use offline.

Tube Deluxe

For the London Underground this is *the* essential app, with network updates, a route finder and offline map.

VIewRanger Outdoors GPS

One of the best apps around for cyclists, walkers, climbers – or any other outdoor types. The in-app purchase mechanism gives you access to offline mapping from a variety of sources, such as Ordnance Survey, OpenStreetMap and OpenCycleMap, and the built-in tools for planning and logging routes are excellent.

World Lens

This is Rough Guides' own home-grown app of inspirational travel photography, with built-in tools for bookmarking and also sharing via email, Facebook and Twitter.

App
essentials

27

Apps: productivity

Tools for everything

Much of this book has looked at the iPad as a device for consuming content – watching video, reading books, and so on. The iPad is well suited to such tasks, but it also has plenty to contribute to getting things done. Here are some of the best tools and utilities to be found in the App Store.

Reminders

Reminders
This built-in app syncs with iCloud (turn It on within Settings > iCloud) and with iCal (Calendar in Mountain Lion) and Outlook. You can also create location-based reminders, so, for example, your iPad may remind you to feed the goldfish when you arrive home.

Remember The Milk

This app is arguably the best task-organizing web-based sync service available right now, though you do have to sign up for a fee-paying Pro account to make use of the iPad app.

GeeTasks

A slick little app for Google Task syncing, complete with a Home Screen badge icon for uncompleted tasks.

OmniFocus

If you like things to be complicated … check in here. The app isn't exactly cheap, but there are no ongoing subscription charges, and with cloud syncing with both the iPhone and Mac versions (all need to be purchased separately) and a ridiculous quantity of customization and task-management tools, you do feel like you're getting your money's worth.

Note-taking apps

Evernote

Evernote can create notes from text, audio and images (any text included in pictures is automatically recognized and, impressively, becomes searchable), and the notes are then synced between whatever desktop and other mobile versions you're also running.

Simplenote

Simplenote is another very good notes and syncing service. It's free to use if you can put up with the ads; if not, sign up for the ad-free, enhanced Simplenote Premium service.

Audio Memos

This is an excellent audio recording app for iPad users. The sound quality is high, and there are lots of filtering, editing and sorting options. If you get really serious, look to the in-app purchases to add compression, voice activation and so on.

Audiotorium

Unlike many note-taking apps, Audiotorium gives you a full set of rich-text functions (bold, italic, etc) and the ability to record hours of audio while also taking text notes, making it great for lectures.

Word processing and writing apps

Pages

Apple's word processing app is slick, but pricey compared to others. It does integrate nicely with iCloud though, meaning you can pick up where you left off on another device.

Doc² (HD)

The formatting tools of this word processor app are really impressive, offering everything from bold, italic and underline to bullets, indents and table construction. But its best feature is that it works with Google Docs to help you share files online.

WriteRoom

Offering a distraction-free writing environment without toolbars or formatting worries, this app also has a nice white-on-black mode that's easy on the eye for extended periods of writing.

Number apps

PCalc Lite & PCalc RPN

You'll be needing a calculator, as the iPad does not have one built in. PCalc Lite is free, looks nice, has scientific functions and can also handle unit conversions. Upgrade to the paid-for PCalc RPN for additional scientific functions and layout options.

Numbers

This iWork application is Apple's answer to Excel. Though not as sophisticated as either the Microsoft desktop program or its own Mac desktop namesake in terms of advanced spreadsheet features, it's nicely put together and does an impressive job of creating both 2D and 3D charts and graphs.

TIP Documents can be uploaded from any of the iWork suite apps (Pages, Numbers, Keynote) to the iCloud website (icloud.com). In any of the apps, view the document gallery, tap **Edit**, highlight a selection, then tap the ↪ icon to see the option of posting to iCloud.

Sheet²

This app crafts fairly impressive spreadsheets and can both edit and create Microsoft Excel documents. It also works with Google Docs for sharing your files online.

TIP If you like the sound of both Sheet² and Doc², check out the Office² app, which combines the two at a cheaper price.

Presentation apps

Keynote

The third member of Apple's iWork toolkit is Keynote: a stylish equivalent of Microsoft's PowerPoint presentation software. What it lacks in features it makes up for in ease of use and elegant templates. It can open and edit PowerPoint documents, and you can also save Keynote projects to iCloud and then download them to a desktop machine as either Keynote, PDF or PowerPoint documents.

TIP Connect your iPad to a projector using a Dock Connector cable or Apple TV and AirPlay, and you can use Keynote to run your presentation as well as to create it.

ProPrompter

With this app you turn your iPad into a script teleprompter and, with the same app installed on another device (iPad, iPhone or iPod touch), you can control the pace of the script on the first device via a Bluetooth connection.

Artistic apps

Brushes

Brushes is a beautifully crafted app that artists of any level can have a lot of fun with. It supports image layering, different brush textures and weights, and the ability to control the transparency and weight of your strokes based on the speed with which you move your finger. It also features a "replay" function that records every brush stroke, letting you play back the progress of your creation.

SketchBook (Mobile & Pro)

Like Brushes, this app supports layers and is really intuitive to use, though it's probably more suited to professionals. It offers loads of tools, brushes and textures, plus an incredible zoom feature that allows you to get right in there to add detail.

123 Color HD

There are loads of colouring apps aimed at kids. This one is a real treat – it has songs, voiceovers and multiple languages built in (so it can be used for basic language teaching too). When they're done, your kids' masterpieces can either be saved to Photos or emailed to granny and grandad.

Whiteboard

Nice app that lets two people on the same Wi-Fi network work on the same piece of art simultaneously.

Draw Something

Holding the record for being one of the fastest growing games ever (fifty million downloads in seven weeks), this collaborative drawing game has you sketching something and, in real time, a remote player trying to guess what it is.

File sharing with apps

Many apps, including the three members of the iWork suite, utilize the File Sharing feature of iTunes as a means of transferring files back and forth between the iPad and your computer. If a particular app supports the feature, it will appear within the **File Sharing** panel in the lower area of the **Apps** tab in iTunes when your iPad is connected. From there you can drag files in (or use the **Add** button to browse for files) and drag files out (or use the **Save to** button to browse for a location to save to). If you would rather share files between your iPad and computer without using iTunes, use an app such as Air Sharing, and, for sharing via the web, Dropbox.

Printing from your iPad

The iPad supports Apple's over-the-airwaves print technology AirPrint, which allows you to send documents, photos, webpages, etc, directly to your printer over a Wi-Fi network. Unfortunately you have to own one of several pricey HP printers to make it work. For a full list of compatible machines, visit hp.com/go/airprint. Once your printer is set up, AirPrint printing is found by tapping the ➦ icon (in many apps), selecting the number of copies you want, and then tapping **Print**.

There are, however, many apps that offer printing functionality without the need to buy a fancy new printer. Both PrinterShare and the delightfully monikered Fax, Print & Share Pro are worth playing with.

If you have a Mac computer with a printer connected to it, then by far the best option is a Mac application called Printopia. Once this application is installed on your computer, your iPad will recognize your printer in the same way it recognizes an AirPrint printer within the ➦ options menu. What's more, the app also allows you to send the print job to your Mac as a JPG or PDF, or if you use Dropbox, directly to your Mac's Dropbox folder. Printopia can be downloaded from ecamm.com/mac/printopia. On a PC a similar result can be acheived using the excellent PrintCentral app and associated WePrint desktop software. Find out more at mobile.eurosmartz.com/downloads/downloads_index.html.

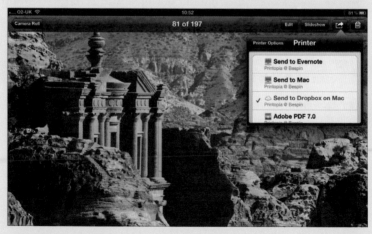

Time

It remains a mystery as to why Apple didn't include a dedicated clock app on the iPad when the iPhone boasts such an excellent built-in timepiece. But not to worry, there are hundreds available in the App Store, and many are free. Here's a handful of the best.

World Clock Pro
This is a great addition to any iPad app collection. The interface is lush and makes it easy to add multiple cities. There are several custom themes and a world map view.

Alarm Clock HD
This is a really well put together nightstand-style alarm clock app, with everything from a Google Reader feed ticker to a music sleep mode.

Timer+
Essential tool for making sure that your roast dinners come together perfectly: it handles multiple timers simultaneously and can handle seconds as well as hours and minutes.

Miscellaneous

Air Display
Turns your iPad into an extra screen for your Mac. Use it, for example, to display a small-window application such as iChat while using your main screen to get on with work.

Airport Utility
This is a very useful app for tweaking the settings of Apple AirPort base-station networks.

Clinometer

There are loads of apps that can act as a spirit level, but this one is particularly well thought through and easy to read.

Convert Units Free HD

The only iPad conversion tool you need: it covers currencies as well as weights, measures, forces, etc.

Data Usage

Get detailed stats and information about the data you are consuming over your cellular network.

iThoughtsHD

A beautiful set of iPad tools for creating mind maps, with loads of export functions and the ability to sync with commonly used services such as Dropbox.

Mood Board

Perfect for project planning, this app gives you a blank canvas on which to pin ideas, text, photos or whatever it is that gets your creative juices flowing. It's easy to use and great for working with colour palettes.

Weather Live

Claiming to be "the most beautiful weather app", Weather Live certainly has a good stab at the title. The animations are delightful, and there are loads of destination search filters and weather parameters to play with.

28

Games

Killing time on the iPad

Playing games on iPads (and iPhones) is so popular that whole new brands have grown up around it – the must-have Angry Birds being an obvious example. Today, over fifty percent of the top-ranking apps in the Store at any one time are games. And it's not just traditional action-packed videogames – blood-splattered zombies and high-octane racing – that are being consumed in vast quantities (though if that's your vice, you won't be disappointed). In this chapter, we'll offer suggestions on everything from fiendishly challenging puzzles to table tennis.

Chess Free (HD)

Dozens of chess apps are available for the iPad. This one is free and does everything you need it to.

Cut The Rope (HD)

A beautifully rendered and often incredibly difficult puzzle game that has you feeding candy to a devilish little green critter. The numerous levels will keep you going for weeks.

Farmville by Zynga

Virtual farming has now become very popular, largely thanks to the viral spread of the Facebook version. The iPad app offers a great experience, but do look out for the in-app purchases, as it's very easy to get carried away with all that Farm Cash.

FIFA 12

It's hard to fathom how they managed to get so much detail and sophisticated gameplay into this iPad game.

Final Fantasy III for iPad

Completely redesigned for iPad gameplay, this classic fantasy adventure has all the excitement and many hours of gameplay of the original (first released way back in 1990).

Flick Kick Football

If you are looking for more of a retro soccer vibe, get your fingers limbered up for this onion-bag-filler.

Galaxy on Fire 2 HD

This processor-heavy science-fiction epic produces an amazing gaming environment. You are taken through a seemingly boundless galaxy of strange worlds and mammoth space stations. Well worth checking out.

Apple Game Center

Apple Game Center is a social-networking tool that many app developers build into their games to enable global leaderboards and multiplayer gameplay. There is also an auto-match feature that can help you find new people to play with. The Game Center app can be found pre-loaded on your iPad; it gives you access to all your scoreboards and also shortcuts to the actual game apps (tap through and hit the Play buttons). Find out more at apple.com/game-center.

Game for Cats

Claiming to be "the first interspecies game on the App Store", this peculiar creation pits your motor skills against those of a feline friend. Cats love it, apparently.

Modern Combat 3: Fallen Nation

The quality of the graphics is jaw-dropping; this really is among the best first-person shooters currently available.

Nano Rally (HD)

This fun racing game sees your tiny vehicle going head to head with other minuscule motors. If you ever played the classic Micro Machines, you'll love this.

Osmos

A mellow cosmic adventure where you battle gravity and mass to "become the biggest" – with a great soundtrack.

Real Racing 2 HD

With thirty cars and fifteen race locations, this is pretty much the best racing game for the iPad right now. There's a special split-screen party mode for playing via AirPlay.

Sonic CD

This beautiful and furious slice of Sonic nostalgia finds our hero battling Dr. Eggman to save Little Planet.

Star Wars Arcade: Falcon Gunner

Re-live the epic dog fight from *Episode IV* between the Millennium Falcon and a squadron of TIE fighters, the asteroid field from *Empire*, and more. Thanks to the iPad's built-in accelerometer you can spin 360 degrees to find and blast your targets: best played on a swivel chair with pets well out of the way.

Temple Run

Picture an endless Indiana Jones chase sequence and you'll get the idea. Run, slide and jump to make your getaway while collecting coins and power-ups.

Whale Trail

This psychedelic maelstrom of thundering clouds, bubbles and fish is pretty wild but at the same time utterly charming. Glide and loop your flying mammal to collect the bubbles.

World Cup Table Tennis (HD)

This ping pong app hooks up with Game Center, so you can battle opponents from around the world.

World of Goo

Beautiful, dark and strange, this game takes you on an adventure through a world of peculiar creatures and bizarre morphing shapes.

TIP The best place to go online for the latest iPad games reviews and news is toucharcade.com. And the forums are very useful for picking up hints and cheats.

Maintenance

29

Resetting & backing up

Troubleshooting and keeping things shipshape

The iPad is basically a computer and, just like its full-sized cousins, it will occasionally crash or become unresponsive. Far less common, and much more serious, is hardware failure, which will require you to send the device away for servicing. This chapter gives advice for both situations, along with tips for maximizing battery life and keeping the screen clean.

Crashes and software problems

You should expect, every now and again, for your iPad to crash or generally behave in strange ways. This will more often than not be a problem with a specific application, and the iPad will simply throw you out of the app and take you back to the Home Screen. From there, remove it from the Multitasking Bar (see p.73), relaunch, and then tap your way back to where you were and start again. If the screen completely freezes, however, try force-quitting the current application by holding down the Home button for about five or six seconds. If the problem persists, try the following steps, in this order:

• **Reboot** As with any other computer, turning an iPad off and back on often solves software problems. Press and hold the **Sleep/Wake** button for a couple of seconds and then slide the red switch to confirm. Count to five; then press and hold the **Sleep/Wake** button again to reboot.

• **Reset** If that doesn't do the trick, or you can't get your iPad to turn off, try resetting. This won't harm any music or data on the device. Press and hold the **Sleep/Wake** button and the **Home** button at the same time for around ten seconds. The iPad may first display the regular shutdown screen and red confirm switch; ignore it, and keep holding the buttons, only letting go when the Apple logo appears.

• **Reset network settings** If the issues you are having are related to connecting to the internet, try this option within **Settings > General > Reset** and then rejoin your prefered Wi-Fi network.

> **TIP** Use the Speedtest X HD app to measure the speed of your iPad's current internet connection; it works for measuring both Wi-Fi and carrier network speeds.

• **Reset all settings** Still no joy? Resetting your iPad's preferences may help. All your current settings will be lost, but no data or media is deleted. Tap **Settings > General > Reset > Reset All Settings**.

• **Erase all content and settings** If that doesn't work, you could try deleting all the media and data, too, by tapping **Settings > General > Reset > Erase All Content and Settings**. Then restore either by connecting to iTunes or wirelessly restoring from an iCloud backup.

• **Restore** You can also restore an unresponsive iPad directly from iTunes (handy if you can't actually get to the **Reset** options mentioned above on the iPad). Connect the iPad to iTunes and, within the **Summary** tab, click **Restore** and follow the prompts.

> **TIP** An iTunes restore will only work if your computer is connected to the internet, as the device needs to be "verified" with the iTunes servers.

• **Software update** You should be prompted to update your iPad's internal software, or operating system, automatically from time to time. But you can check for new versions at any time from the **Settings > General > Software Update** screen. This can also be done within iTunes by clicking the **Check for Update** button on the **Summary** tab when your iPad is highlighted in the sidebar. If a new version is available, be sure to install it.

Backing up

It is important to maintain a backup of the data, settings and configuration of your iPad, including your mail settings, sound settings and other preferences. From a saved backup, you can restore your device to its previous state should it need to be reset to factory settings. A backup can also help you to set up a new iPad with the same configuration as an older device as and when you upgrade to a newer model. There are two ways to set up automatic backups:

Backing up to iCloud

Look within **Settings > iCloud > Storage & Backup** and slide the iCloud Backup switch to the **On** position. Alternatively, connect to iTunes and look for the option under the **Summary** tab. To see how much of your iCloud storage space is being consumed by the backup, tap **Settings** > **iCloud** > **Storage & Backup** > **Manage Storage**. Next, tap through to see exactly what's being backed up from your device. There is a separate listing for every app and you can choose to stop backing up specific apps if you wish (perhaps if an app is taking up a lot of space).

> **TIP** Note the green strip at the bottom of the screen that displays how much of your iCloud quota is left. If you need more storage space, tap the **Buy More Storage** button.

Backing up to iTunes

To back up to iTunes on your computer, connect your iPad and look under the **Summary** tab in iTunes for the option **Back up to this computer**. You can also set an encryption password so that those with access to your computer will not be able to restore their devices to your backup and overwrite it.

To view, and if necessary delete, an automatic iPad backup in iTunes, open **iTunes Preferences** and click **Devices**. Of course, a backup stored in iTunes rather than iCloud is only as safe as your Mac or PC. Computers can die, get destroyed or be stolen, so get into the habit of backing up your computer to either an external hard drive or cloud-based computer backup service.

Automatic and manual backups

If you use the iCloud method, your backup will be automatically updated whenever your iPad is plugged in, locked and connected to Wi-Fi. While connected to Wi-Fi you can also manually kick-start a backup via the **Settings** > **iCloud** > **Storage & Backup** screen.

An iTunes backup will happen automatically whenever your iPad is connected to iTunes via either a cable or your Wi-Fi network. To set it going manually, right-click on your iPad in the iTunes sidebar and select the option to **Back Up**.

30

Batteries & repairs

Energy tips and getting fixed

Like all lithium-ion batteries, the one inside the iPad lasts for a certain amount of time before starting to lose its ability to hold a full charge. According to Apple, this reduction in capacity of a "properly maintained" iPad battery will happen after around one thousand "charge cycles" – which, in theory, should give you a good few years of usage, assuming you charge the device on average once a day.

Once the battery has reached the end of its useful life, you can pay to have the battery replaced (though Apple claim that they will in fact replace the entire device). For the full story, see: apple.com/support/ipad/service/battery and then click the **Battery Replacement** link. If, on the other hand, you drain your battery twice a day by watching movies while commuting to and from work, you might see your battery deteriorate after just nine months or so. In this case, you'd get it replaced for free, as the iPad would still be within warranty.

If the battery won't charge

There has been a fair amount of controversy, and no shortage of misinformation, about issues iPad owners have had trying to charge their devices via a USB port on Macs, PCs and USB hubs. If your iPad won't charge up via a USB port, it could be that the port you're connected to doesn't supply enough power or that your Mac or PC is going into standby mode during the charge.

It has also been reported that iPads charge differently in sleep and wake modes from certain USB ports. To test this hypothesis for your USB port, note the percentage charge on the Status Bar before you connect; then if you see the infuriating "Not charging" message on the iPad's Status Bar, press the Sleep/Wake button to darken the screen and then head to the kettle. Return after a cup of tea, disconnect, and see if the charge has increased.

If you still have no joy, make sure the iPad is working properly by trying to charge via the supplied power adapter. If this doesn't work either, it could be the cable; if you have an iPhone or iPod cable lying around, try that instead, or borrow one from a friend. If you still can't get it to charge, send the iPad for servicing.

Tips for maximizing battery life

Below, you'll find various techniques for minimizing the demands on your iPad battery. Each one will help ensure that your charge lasts for as long as possible and that your battery's overall lifespan is maximized.

• **Keep it cool** Avoid leaving your iPad in direct sunlight or anywhere hot. Apple state that the device works best at 0–35°C (32–95°F). As a general rule, try to keep it at room temperature.

• **Keep it updated** One of the things that software updates can help with is battery efficiency. So accept any that are offered (see p.258).

• **Drain it** As with all lithium-ion batteries, it's a good idea to run your iPad completely flat once a month and then fully charge it again.

• **Dim it** Screen brightness makes a big difference to battery life, so if you think you could live with less of it, turn down the slider within **Settings** > **Brightness & Wallpaper**. Experiment with and without the **Auto-Brightness** option, which adjusts screen brightness according to ambient light levels.

• **Quit multitasking apps** Any apps that are doing their own thing in the background will be draining your battery, so if your battery is low, clear the Multitasking Bar (see p.73).

• **Turn off notifications** Head to **Settings** > **Notifications** and turn off notifications for any apps you really don't need to be hearing from.

• **Tweak your Fetch settings** Within **Settings** > **Mail, Contacts, Calendars** > **Fetch New Data**, turn **Push** to off and choose to **Fetch Manually** (i.e., when you open the Mail or Calendar apps) or **Hourly**.

• **Turn off Location Services** As above, if you need to conserve energy when out and about, turning this off (**Settings** > **Location Services**) will really help to extend your charge.

• **Lock it** Press the Sleep/Wake button when you're not using the iPad to avoid wasting energy. Many iPad cases (such as the Apple Smart Cover) will automatically lock and power-down the screen when closed if the option is enabled within **Settings** > **General**, meaning you don't have to be so vigilant about using the Sleep/Wake button.

• **Turn off Wi-Fi, Cellular Data & Bluetooth** These power-hungry connections are easily turned off when not in use. Use the switches under **Settings** > **Wi-Fi, Settings** > **Cellular Data**, and **Settings** > **General** > **Bluetooth**.

• **Junk the EQ in the Music app** Set your iPad to use Flat EQ settings (under **Settings** > **Music**). This will knock out imported iTunes EQ settings, which can increase battery demands.

• **Stay lo-fi** High-bitrate music formats such as Apple Lossless may improve the sound quality (see p.152), but they also increase the power required for playback. If you sync your music from iTunes, look for the option under the **Summary** tab to **Convert higher bit rate songs to 128, 192 and 256 kbps**. Any of these options is going to be more battery efficient than Apple Lossless, so feel free to go for 256 kbps (which is the bitrate you get with iTunes Store purchases).

> **TIP** For Apple's full list of iPad battery preservation tips, visit their website: apple.com/batteries/ipad.html.

iPad repairs

If the troubleshooting advice in this book hasn't worked, try going online and searching for help in the sites and forums listed on p.264. If that doesn't clear things up, it could be that you'll need to have your iPad repaired by Apple. To do this, you could take it to an Apple retail store (see p.46), though you may have to make an appointment.

Alternatively, visit the following website and fill out a service request form. Apple will send you an addressed box in which you can return your iPad to them. It will arrive back by post.

Apple Self-Solve selfsolve.apple.com

Either way, you're advised to remove your SIM card (if your iPad has one) before sending it off and you can choose to hire a replacement iPad for the period of repair. But make sure you return it on time, or you'll be charged a fee, or the full price of the iPad, depending on the length of the delay.

Warranty, AppleCare+ and insurance

The iPad comes with a one-year warranty that covers everything you'd expect (hardware failure and so on) and nothing that you wouldn't (accidents, loss, theft and unauthorized service). In addition, you can choose to extend your warranty by a further two years through the AppleCare+ scheme. The price at the time of writing is $99 (£61 for the AppleCare Protection Plan in the UK). This service includes battery cover and two accidental damage repairs (with a $49 surcharge) – which could be handy if you're prone to screen breakages.

AppleCare apple.com/support/products

As for insurance against accidental damage and theft, most network carriers in most countries do offer insurance, albeit for a fairly high fee. Alternatively, you could investigate what options are available via your home contents scheme. Many insurers offer away-from-home coverage for high-value items – though this can also be expensive.

Useful websites

If you have an ailing iPad, or if you want the latest tips, tap Safari and drop in to one of these support sites or forums…

Apple Support apple.com/support/ipad/

Apple Forums discussions.apple.com

iPad Forums ipadforums.net

EverythingiCafe everythingicafe.com/forum

If you're the kind of person who likes to take things apart, check out the "Cracking Open the Apple iPad" article at TechRepublic, and follow up with one of the numerous "iPad disassembly" or "iPad mod" posts on YouTube. Trying any such thing at home will, of course, thoroughly void your warranty.

TechRepublic techrepublic.com

YouTube youtube.com (or use the built-in app, see p.186)

Useful apps

System Status
This is a useful app for monitoring your iPad's systems. Some of the data it delivers is a bit nerdy, but it does offer some handy features such as notifications when your battery is fully charged.

Battery
There are loads of apps that can display in detail how much time you have left to do different activities based on your current charge. This is one of the more handsome.

SYS Activity Manager
Another fully featured utility for monitoring current iPad system activity. With readouts for RAM status, cellular activity and a nice storage visualization too, it's worth trying out the free version (alternatively, go for the paid app to lose the ads).

> **TIP** If you have a suggestion about how the iPad could be improved, then tell Apple at: apple.com/feedback/ipad.html

Index

P